Ken Boa never writes a predictable book. Everything I've read surprises me, catches me off guard, and opens new awareness of thought. Leadership is a worn out topic, but when addressed by Dr. Boa, it comes alive.

DR. LARRY CRABB
CHRISTIAN COUNSELOR, NEW WAY MINISTRIES AND SOUL CARE MINISTRIES

I have had the privilege of knowing Ken Boa for quite some time. He is one of the most consistent followers of Jesus Christ that I know. As such, he is uniquely capable and gifted to write on *The Perfect Leader*, God. This book will challenge any leader to examine his life to see whether or not he is striving to attain Godly character. It will be an encouragement to anyone wanting to become a more effective leader. I recommend it without reservation, wholeheartedly and enthusiastically.

RON BLUE
CPA, FOUNDER OF RON BLUE & CO., LLC

There is deep wisdom in this book for both new and seasoned leaders. Ken Boa derives leadership traits from the very ground of all goodness and truth: the nature and character of God. From that starting point he calls the reader to repentance and faith and to the great adventure of leading others.

CHUCK COLSON
FOUNDER AND CHAIRMAN, PRISON FELLOWSHIP

Many books in the Christian market attempt to take accepted business principles and find their correlation to Scripture. *The Perfect Leader* begins with God himself as the ultimate model of leadership. The underlying premise is that throughout the Bible, God has demonstrated principles for leadership that can be profitably used by all people who are in a position to lead others—whether in business or ministry, in the school or in the home.

HOWARD HENDRICKS
DALLAS THEOLOGICAL SEMINARY/BIBLICAL DISCERNMENT MINISTRIES

I love to read Ken Boa's books, and this book is no exception. *The Perfect Leader* maximizes Ken's great strengths of biblical scholarship, clear thinking, refreshing humor, and specific application. In a landscape glutted with material on leadership, what a refreshing and inspiring idea to use God himself as the model for leadership. I highly recommend you read this book and then use the excellent questions provided for each chapter to develop the leaders around you.

CHIP INGRAM
PRESIDENT, WALK THRU THE BIBLE
TEACHING PASTOR, LIVING ON THE EDGE

Character is definitive in the realm of leadership; it is not simply about being obedient to the claims of God upon your life, but rather determining your very motives and what spurs you to service and action. Echoing this theme, Ken Boa examines the heart of God—his passion and purpose—and re⌐⌐ ⌐w God himself is the ultimate model of a leader. As a skillful ⌐⌐⌐ ⌐⌐⌐ presents case studies of very human biblical lead⌐⌐ to God, so that we might integrate these criti⌐

ZACHARIAS
⌐INISTRIES

I have known Dr. Boa for a number of years as a man deeply committed to the things of Christ. He combines a first class mind with a firm grasp of Scripture, filtered through a tender heart for God. I highly commend him to you.

WALTER A. HENRICHSEN
PRESIDENT, LEADERSHIP FOUNDATION

Kenneth D. Boa is faithful in his exposition of the Word and skillful in his defense of the faith delivered to the saints. His ministry will prove to be enlightening and encouraging. He is trustworthy in handling the Scriptures and convincing in its application to life.

J. DWIGHT PENTECOST
PROFESSOR EMERITUS, DALLAS THEOLOGICAL SEMINARY

Dr. Boa's solid and stimulating presentation of spiritual truths will certainly profit all who are privileged to sit under his ministry.

CHARLES C. RYRIE
PROFESSOR EMERITUS, DALLAS THEOLOGICAL SEMINARY
EDITOR OF THE BEST-SELLING RYRIE STUDY BIBLE

I have known Ken Boa since 1968. During all this time he has exhibited a constancy of Christian character and excellence in service to God. His exceptional ability in explaining God's Word is evident in his teaching and writing.

HAROLD W. HOEHNER
CHAIR, NEW TESTAMENT, DALLAS THEOLOGICAL SEMINARY

Ken Boa has a lot to say. His personal conversion to Christ is remarkable—a testimony to God's grace—and his message is both biblical and relevant. Ken is both a scholar and a man who speaks to people in a very practical and personal way, which is reflected in his literature. His writings will help any Christian to develop a more intimate relationship with Jesus Christ.

GENE A. GETZ
FOUNDER OF FELLOWSHIP BIBLE CHURCH NORTH, AUTHOR, AND RADIO HOST

The Lord has gifted Ken Boa with a unique blend of intellectual and relational gifts to carry God's Word to spiritually hungry people. Ken's deep desire to know the Lord and to make him known is evident throughout his writing and teaching. I would highly recommend Ken and his ministry to you and I know that you will be blessed and encouraged.

JOSEPH M. STOWELL
FORMER PRESIDENT OF MOODY BIBLE INSTITUTE,
PASTOR OF HARVEST BIBLE CHAPEL IN ILLINOIS

THE
PERFECT
LEADER

KENNETH BOA

Victor®

The Bible Teacher's Teacher

COOK COMMUNICATIONS MINISTRIES
Colorado Springs, Colorado • Paris, Ontario
KINGSWAY COMMUNICATIONS LTD
Eastbourne, England

Victor® is an imprint of
Cook Communications Ministries, Colorado Springs, CO 80918
Cook Communications, Paris, Ontario
Kingsway Communications, Eastbourne, England

THE PERFECT LEADER
© 2006 by Kenneth Boa

Cover Design: BMB Design
Cover Photo: BigStockPhoto.com

First Printing, 2006
Printed in the United States of America

2 3 4 5 6 7 8 9 10

Library of Congress Cataloging-in-Publication Data

Boa, Kenneth.
  The perfect leader : practicing the leadership traits of God / Kenneth
Boa.
      p. cm.
  Includes bibliographical references.
  ISBN 978-0-7814-4272-5
  1. Leadership--Religious aspects--Christianity. 2. Leadership--Biblical
teaching. I. Title.
  BV4597.53.L43.B63 2005
  253--dc22
                                          2005029525

Dedication

To Steve and Elyse Harvey Lawson,
beloved friends of Karen and mine for many years.

Acknowledgment

With gratitude to John and Jill Turner
for their significant work on this project, and
to Sid Buzzell and Bill Perkins for our association in
creating The Leadership Bible.

Contents

Introduction

Generally speaking, leaders are readers. Most leaders are well read on the subject of effective leadership. Books written by successful leaders are in no short supply. In fact, the publishing market is well stocked with books, magazines, and other materials by countless experts who offer their own philosophy and principles on dealing with the challenges and opportunities facing anyone who will dare step out of the crowd and assume the mantle of leadership.

Many books in the Christian market attempt to take accepted business principles and find their correlation to Scripture. *The Perfect Leader* begins with God himself as the ultimate model of leadership. The underlying premise is that, throughout the Bible, God has demonstrated principles for leadership that can be used profitably by all people who are in a position to lead others—whether in business or ministry, in the school or in the home.

In short, this book will help you develop a heart for effective leadership by developing a heart for God. It will encourage you to develop a leadership style that is based on the character and nature of God and the timeless, eternal truths found in his Word—all this while your love and admiration for him increase.

Each chapter in the book does four things: (1) introduces the principle to be discussed, providing you new insight on the well-known principle; (2) focuses on a particular attribute of God as the basis for the leadership principle; (3) prompts self-examination as it guides you to explore your own position in relation to the leadership principle being addressed;

and (4) provides an in-depth look at how the leadership principle works when it is executed in a biblically directed way. Each chapter draws on the insights of numerous leadership experts and, of course, biblical teaching.

The Perfect Leader uses some of the categories that Sid Buzzell, Bill Perkins, and I developed when we created *The Leadership Bible* (Zondervan, 1998). We are convinced that these principles and categories will help you learn to be a leader in the image of God.

Part 1:

THE ATTRIBUTES OF THE PERFECT LEADER

CHAPTER 1

Integrity

I AM WHO I AM

After surveying thousands of people around the world and preparing more than four hundred written case studies, James Kouzes and Barry Posner identified those characteristics most desired in a leader. In virtually every survey, honesty or integrity was identified more frequently than any other trait.[1]

That makes sense. If people are going to follow someone, whether into battle or in business or ministry, they want assurance that their leader can be trusted. They want to know that person will keep promises and follow through with commitments.

Promises and commitments are significant, even though, in our day of Machiavellian ethics, it seems that they have become optional. We often seem more concerned with convenience and performance. We give lip service to the importance of character, but we have the idea that when things get tough, the rules can be changed and commitments and covenants may be discarded at will.

But the Bible makes clear just how important covenants are. Throughout the Scriptures, God focuses on the fact that he is a God who makes and keeps his covenants, that he can be trusted (1 Chronicles 16:15; Psalm 105:8). God can be trusted because he is trustworthy. That is the point: it always comes down to the issue of character, not just words. Biblical integrity is not just a matter of doing the right thing; it is a matter of having the right heart and allowing the person on the inside to match the person on the outside. This is how God is. This is how his people should be.

Perhaps a good word to describe this trait of integrity is "consistency." There must be consistency between what is inside and what is outside. God is totally consistent. His actions and behaviors always match his character and nature. And his goal for his children is nothing less. Christ's desire for his disciples is that they be disciplined people. In the words of John Ortberg, "Disciplined people can do the right thing at the right time in the right way for the right reason."[2] Just like God.

THE GOD WHO NEVER CHANGES

Is there anyone we can trust? People let us down again and again, because there is often a discrepancy between what they claim to believe and how they actually live. But God will never let us down, because he never changes. His promises are as good as his unchanging character: "Jesus Christ is the same yesterday and today and forever" (Hebrews 13:8).

Jesus does not change. The living God does not change. Neither his love, nor his truth, nor his goodness are governed by external circumstances or conditions—they never vacillate. Therefore, God's character and the promises he makes are supremely worthy of trust and commitment. He does what he says, and his covenant love is always dependable.

This consistency and trustworthiness is fundamental. What else can we lean against? What else can we trust in? What else can we pursue with reckless abandon? So many of us have been burned by relationships, by people going back on their word, claiming that they said something when they did not say it, or that they did not say something when they did. It can make us cynical if we are not careful. But when we come back to the character of God, we realize that he is the unchanging standard.

Because it is impossible for God to lie (Hebrews 6:18; Titus 1:2), he is the ultimately reliable source of hope. His changeless character is the foundation of all of his promises. Whatever he says he will do is as good as done, and when we hope in his promises, this hope becomes an anchor for the soul, both firm and secure (Hebrews 6:19). Unlike many executives, God's yes is always yes, and his no is always no (James 5:12). When God says yes, it stays yes; when he says no, it stays no. This reliability has both negative and positive ramifications. Negatively, there is no getting God to change his mind through bribery or whining. Positively, when God makes a promise, he can be counted on to fulfill that word.

The sting remains of broken promises from bosses—raises never given, promotions never realized, benefits never provided. The writer of Proverbs accurately diagnoses much of our present malaise when he says, "Hope deferred makes the heart sick" (Proverbs 13:12). Much of the heartache we experience is directly related to the unreliability of people.

But God's actions flow perfectly out of his character: "He who is the Glory of Israel does not lie or change his mind; for he is not a man, that he should change his mind" (1 Samuel 15:29). There is no possibility of manipulating or bribing or bargaining with God, because he will never compromise his perfect integrity. God himself has testified, "I the LORD do not change" (Malachi 3:6). God's perfect and constant character allows us to trust in his promises and timing.

God *is* integrity. He does not merely act with integrity; integrity is his character. But what about us? The biblical virtue of integrity points to a consistency between what is inside and what is outside, between belief and behavior, between our words and our ways, our attitudes and our actions, our values and our practices.

THE PROCESS OF INTEGRATION

It is self-evident that a hypocrite is unqualified to guide others toward attaining higher character. No one respects a person who talks a good game but fails to play by the rules. What a leader does will have a greater impact on those he wishes to lead than what he says. A person may forget 90 percent of what a leader says, but he will never forget how the leader lives. This is why Paul told Timothy:

> Be diligent in these matters; give yourself wholly to them, so that everyone may see your progress. Watch your life and doctrine closely. Persevere in them, because if you do, you will save both yourself and your hearers. (1 Timothy 4:15–16)

In this life, we will never attain perfection. But we should be making continual progress toward the upward call of God in Christ Jesus (Philippians 3:14). We will never attain it this side of eternity, but there should be visible progress, evident to others. Notice the two things Paul exhorted Timothy to watch: his life and his doctrine. In other words, Paul was telling Timothy, "Give careful attention to your behavior and your belief. Make sure they match. Constantly examine yourself to see whether your walk matches your talk."

Bill Hendricks encountered an illustration of this principle in the go-go days of the real estate market of the 1980s. He met a developer who claimed to have woven what he called "biblical principles of business" into his deals. But when the market went sour, he skipped town and left his investors to pick up the pieces—and pay off the debts.

Another of Bill's friends stood in sharp contrast to the first. He too was a land developer. He too talked of integrating biblical principles into his business. And when the market crashed, so did his empire. But unlike the man who ran away, this land developer, as a matter of conscience, worked out a plan to pay back his investors.[3]

Money tends to bring out what's really inside. When it comes to financial matters, we discover what a person is made of. Which of those two men would you rather follow? Which one demonstrated integrity? David wrote about the man "who keeps his oath even when it hurts" (Psalm 15:4). He is the man who "will never be shaken" (v. 5). There is simply no substitute for a person of consistent Christlike character.

That doesn't mean that any of us will ever be sinless in this life. In fact, the New Testament doesn't call for flawless leaders; it calls for those who are *models of progress in their faith*. So why then in Jesus' Sermon on the Mount did he call his followers to "be perfect, therefore, as your heavenly Father is perfect" (Matthew 5:48)? Clearly in this physical existence we cannot claim to be without sin (see 1 John 1:8).

Actually, what Jesus is calling us to is the process of being perfected, rather than completing our perfection (this side of eternity, anyway). It's the sanctifying work of God's Holy Spirit in the life of the believing leader that does the perfecting. We all will continue to stumble in many ways, but our desire should be about cooperating with God to see progress toward the integration of our claims and our practice. Because it's only the perfecting process of God (the truly perfect leader) at work in us that can accomplish any real progress.

Secrecy and Small Things

The best way to discern whether or not we are making progress is to ask ourselves, "How do I live when no one's looking?" It is easy to look like a person of integrity when people are watching, but do we live our private lives with the same level of consistency that we live our public lives? So much of our lives is consumed with what might be called "image maintenance." We spend vast amounts of energy trying to get people to think about us the way we want to be thought about. John Ortberg suggests, "Human conversation is largely an endless attempt to convince others that we are more assertive or clever or gentle or successful than they might think if we did not carefully educate them."[4] Jesus' words in Matthew 6:1 are hard to get around: "Be careful not to do your 'acts of righteousness' before men, to be seen by them. If you do, you will have no reward from your Father in heaven."

It is possible to live one life publicly and another life privately. That is not integrity; it is an invitation for God's discipline. We are to live with consistency in public and in private, because our Father "sees what is done in secret" (Matthew 6:4). Since this is the case, being faithful in small, secret things is a big deal. It may be that God is far less concerned with our public personas than he is with our private characters. He may be more concerned with how we manage our personal checking accounts than he is with how well we administer the books of a huge business concern. It is in the small, secret places of self-evaluation that God's grace changes us and shapes us into the image of his Son (2 Corinthians 3:18).

In the end, we become what our desires make us. Who we become reveals what we really desire. If we desire the praise of others, then we will become a certain kind of person. But if we desire the praise of God, then we need to make integrity a priority in our lives. As we sense the overwhelming holiness of our Creator, we will understand how unraveled we are. But as we focus on the grace of our Lord and Savior Jesus Christ, we will recognize that even though we may feel undone, we are not undone because he has made us whole. His grace is sufficient, for his power is made perfect in our weakness (2 Corinthians 12:9).

The Dis-integration of Isaiah

When the prophet Isaiah had a vision of the glorious and awesome Creator of the universe, he was overwhelmed by the holiness of God:

> In the year that King Uzziah died, I saw the LORD
> seated on a throne, high and exalted, and the train of

his robe filled the temple. Above him were seraphs, each with six wings: With two wings they covered their faces, with two they covered their feet, and with two they were flying. And they were calling to one another:

"Holy, holy, holy is the LORD Almighty; the whole earth is full of his glory."

At the sound of their voices the doorposts and thresholds shook and the temple was filled with smoke.

"Woe to me!" I cried. "I am ruined [undone, KJV]! For I am a man of unclean lips, and I live among a people of unclean lips, and my eyes have seen the King, the LORD Almighty."

Then one of the seraphs flew to me with a live coal in his hand, which he had taken with tongs from the altar. With it he touched my mouth and said, "See, this has touched your lips; your guilt is taken away and your sin atoned for." (Isaiah 6:1–7)

R. C. Sproul comments on Isaiah's encounter with the holiness of God:

> To be undone means to come apart at the seams, to be unraveled. What Isaiah was expressing is what modern psychologists describe as the experience of personal disintegration. To disintegrate means exactly what the word suggests, "dis integrate." To integrate something is to put pieces together in a unified whole.... The word integrity ... [suggests] a person whose life is whole or wholesome. In modern slang we say, "He's got it all together."[5]

Isaiah said, "I'm undone. I'm torn apart," which is just the opposite of integrity. To have integrity is to be integrated, to be whole, to have it all together in a sense, to be consistent. Isaiah found himself torn apart, and this condition forced him to realize his own deficiency. When faced with the awesome holiness of God, Isaiah became aware of his own uncleanness.

When we live our entire lives before the face of God (*corem deo*) and practice a constant abiding in his presence, we realize that being people who do not manifest integrity is inconsistent with the dignity and destiny to which we have been called. As believers, we are to "live a life worthy of the calling [we] have received" (Ephesians 4:1), because, now, Christ is in us. He wants to live his life through us (Galatians 2:20); we are not only his representatives (2 Corinthians 5:20), as members of his church we are, in some mysterious way, his body (Ephesians 1:23; Colossians 1:24).

Now, that is impossible unless he dwells in us, but therein lies the solution. In fact, this is the genius of the Christian life. Christianity is not a religion; it is a relationship. Christianity is not a list of rules and regulations. Instead, it is the presence and power of a person who indwells us and promises never to leave us or forsake us (Hebrews 13:5).

As fallen men and women, we realize how disintegrated we are when we come face to face with God's perfect integration. And, like Isaiah, that confrontation forces us to recognize our deep need for personal reconstruction. Isaiah realized the depth of his own sin in the process of catching a glimpse of God's perfect holiness, and he acknowledged those areas in which he had turned from his commitments as a priest and a prophet. But his commitment and his life as a faithful prophet demonstrate for us the possibility of framing a life of integrity with God's help.

The Hypocrisy of the Pharisees

If we fail to face up to our inadequacy, we fall into the trap of the Pharisees: hypocrisy. Hypocrisy is the opposite of integrity. In Matthew 23, Jesus repeatedly accused the Pharisees and teachers of the law of hypocrisy. Six times in this chapter, he used the stinging word "hypocrites" (vv. 13, 15, 23, 25, 27, 29). Originally, a hypocrite was an actor who put on a mask to assume a false identity while he played for the audience. This accusation would have been particularly offensive to the Pharisees who hated all forms of Hellenization (Greek influence and culture), including the Greek theater. In essence, Jesus was calling them the very thing they hated.

Anyone who has ever labored under the false notion that Jesus was some kind of quiet, nice man will have trouble with these verses:

> Woe to you, teachers of the law and Pharisees, you hypocrites! You travel over land and sea to win a single convert, and when he becomes one, you make him twice as much a son of hell as you are....
> Woe to you, teachers of the law and Pharisees, you hypocrites! You are like whitewashed tombs, which look beautiful on the outside but on the inside are full of dead men's bones and everything unclean. In the same way, on the outside you appear to people as righteous but on the inside you are full of hypocrisy and wickedness....
> You snakes! You brood of vipers! How will you escape being condemned to hell? (Matthew 23:15, 27–28, 33)

This Jesus is not, to use Philip Yancey's expression, "Mr. Rogers with a beard!" Jesus' language reveals the depth of his righteous anger. Notice that each verse that includes the word "hypocrite" begins with the words "Woe to you." This word "woe" (Gr., *ouai*) can contain pathos, anger, warning, and derision; and it may include all of these at the same time. In this passage, Jesus lambasted the Pharisees for saying one thing and doing another. Not only was their lack of integrity substandard for would-be followers of Christ, as religious leaders they were guilty of misrepresenting God the Father.

We have already discovered that integrity—the direct opposite of hypocrisy—is the quality that people want most in a leader. Clearly, the Pharisees and teachers of the law in Jesus' day failed to live up to that standard. When we talk about integrity today, we generally use other, closely related terms such as *ethics* and *morality*. But a clear understanding of the concept of *integrity* requires clear thinking about all three words. Each has a distinct meaning. When properly used, they bring clarity to a crucial but often misunderstood leadership essential:

> *Ethics* refers to a standard of right and wrong, good and evil. It is what the Pharisees *said* they believed was right.
>
> *Morality* is a lived standard of right and wrong, good and evil. It is what the Pharisees actually *did*.

To have integrity is to be sound, complete, integrated. To the extent that a person's ethics and morality are integrated, that person has integrity. To the extent that a person's ethics and morality are not integrated, that person lacks integrity.

Let's look at this another way. If one of our friends tells us that he will lie, cheat, and steal, he has low ethics. If he does business that way, he also has low morality. He is unethical and immoral, but he has integrity—twisted as it may be—because his morality is consistent with his ethics. If he claims to cheat and steal but doesn't cheat and steal, he is moral in practice but he lacks integrity, because his morality doesn't match his ethics.

The Bible teaches high and holy ethics. If we claim to be Christians and to live by biblical standards, we are making an ethical statement. We are committing ourselves to a certain morality. For us to have integrity, then, we must live by biblical ethics. Jesus makes it unequivocally clear that the worst choice is the hypocritical one. This is serious business. When we find our walk not matching our talk, the probing question of Jesus should echo in our hearts: "Why do you call me, 'Lord, Lord,' and do not do what I say?" (Luke 6:46). If we imagine the holy eyes of Jesus Christ, Lord of the universe, as he asks this question, we ought to be at least a little frightened.

THE INTEGRITY OF SAMUEL

In light of this definition of integrity, Israel's high regard for the prophet Samuel should come as no surprise. Samuel was a man who exuded integrity. Nowhere is this fact better illustrated than in 1 Samuel 12:1–4:

> Samuel said to all Israel, "I have listened to everything you said to me and have set a king over you. Now you have a king as your leader. As for me, I am old and gray, and my sons are here with you. I have been your leader from my youth until this day. Here I stand. Testify against me in the presence of the LORD and his anointed. Whose ox have I taken? Whose donkey have I taken? Whom have I cheated? Whom have I oppressed? From whose hand have I accepted a bribe to make me shut my eyes? If I have done any of these, I will make it right."
> "You have not cheated or oppressed us," they replied. "You have not taken anything from anyone's hand."

During his farewell speech, after having led Israel for decades, Samuel promised to repay anything he had unjustly taken from anyone. What a promise! Even more impressive was the people's response. Not one person rose up to make a claim against Samuel.

Samuel's honesty and personal integrity permeated every area of his life. These two characteristics directed the way he regarded his possessions, his business dealings, and his treatment of those who were weaker than he was. Samuel held himself accountable to the people he led. He opened himself up to the scrutiny of everyone with whom he had ever had dealings. As a result of this practice, Samuel's leadership has become legendary as this story has been told and retold throughout the centuries.

CHOOSE THIS DAY

We can have high or low ethics. We can be moral or immoral. The choice is ours. But if we want to have integrity, we must choose our ethics and live to match them. If we want to lead others, we at least owe it to our prospective followers to let them know what they are getting into when they choose us as their leaders.

1. James M. Kouzes and Barry Z. Posner, *Credibility: How Leaders Gain and Lose It, Why People Demand It* (San Francisco: Jossey-Bass, 1993), 14.
2. John Ortberg, *The Life You've Always Wanted* (Grand Rapids, MI: Zondervan, 1997), 55.
3. Adapted from Howard Hendricks and William Hendricks, *As Iron Sharpens Iron* (Chicago: Moody Press, 1995), 67–69.
4. Ortberg, *The Life You've Always Wanted*, 164.
5. R. C. Sproul, *One Holy Passion* (Nashville: Thomas Nelson Publishers, 1987).

CHAPTER 2

Character

WISDOM FOR DUMMIES

People generally don't like being called "dummies." And yet how can we explain the overwhelming success of a series of books aimed at dummies? Beginning with the November 1991 publication of *DOS for Dummies*, the series now has more than one hundred million copies in print, dealing with everything from exercise and nutrition to managing finances to planning a European vacation.

From the very beginning, the concept was simple but powerful: relate to the anxiety and frustration that people feel about technology by making fun of it through books that are educational and humorous—books that make difficult material interesting and easy. Throw in a dash of personality and some entertaining cartoons and—presto—a ... *for Dummies* book!

The Old Testament book of Proverbs does much the same thing (minus the cartoons). It takes the timeless wisdom of God and makes it easy to understand for regular people with no theological training. The book of Proverbs could be called *Wisdom for Dummies*.

The Old Testament proverbs were collected and written down to help us make one of the most vital and basic choices in life—the choice between wisdom and folly, between walking with God and walking on our own. In the book of Proverbs both wisdom and folly are described as people who walk through the streets of the city and call out to us, hawking their wares and beckoning us to taste a sample (Proverbs 1:10–33). Solomon, who is credited with authoring the book of Proverbs, provides us with an excellent jumping-off point for developing the character qualities essential to good leadership:

> My son, if you accept my words and store up my
> commands within you, turning your ear to wisdom
> and applying your heart to understanding, and if you
> call out for insight and cry aloud for understanding,
> and if you look for it as for silver and search for it as
> for hidden treasure, then you will understand the
> fear of the LORD and find the knowledge of God. For
> the LORD gives wisdom, and from his mouth come
> knowledge and understanding. He holds victory in
> store for the upright, he is a shield to those whose
> walk is blameless, for he guards the course of the just
> and protects the way of his faithful ones.
>
> Then you will understand what is right and just
> and fair—every good path. For wisdom will enter
> your heart, and knowledge will be pleasant to your
> soul. Discretion will protect you, and understanding
> will guard you. (Proverbs 2:1–11)

Leaders cultivate character by acquiring wisdom and understanding. Of course, those possessions don't come without a price. They require the kind of dedicated and patient labor exercised in mining for gold and silver. Leaders must diligently "search" for the wisdom that is buried within God's Word like treasure covered by layers of earth and rock. That means using the right tools and exercising patience and diligence as we spend time immersed within this life-changing book. As Marjorie Thompson writes, "It would be nice if we could simply 'practice the presence of God' in all of life, without expending energy on particular exercises. But the capacity to remember and abide in God's presence comes only through steady training."[1] We cannot pay someone else to develop our character strength any more than we can pay someone to develop physical muscles for us. If we want to grow stronger, we have to push the weight ourselves.

Neither can we expect to have a muscular character overnight. It requires effort and time. Douglas J. Rumford says, "Character is like physical exercise or any form of learning; you cannot 'cram,' hoping to do in a day or week what can only be accomplished by months and years of consistent practice."[2] This is why the writer of Proverbs uses words that call his readers to energetic and passionate action.

As we dig, we must ask God to provide us with insight and understanding. Ultimately, only God can open our eyes to see spiritual truth and then enable us to apply that truth to our lives (Ephesians 1:18). As God fills our mind with wisdom, our character will develop so that we will possess the ability to consistently make right choices—choices that are just, fair, and moral. As Henry Blackaby and Claude King note in their book *Experiencing God:*

> Once you come to believe God, you demonstrate
> your faith by what you do. Some action is
> required.... You cannot continue life as usual or stay
> where you are, and go with God at the same time....
> To go from your ways, thoughts, and purposes to
> God's will always requires a major adjustment. God
> may require adjustments in your circumstances, rela-
> tionships, thinking, commitments, actions, and
> beliefs. Once you have made the necessary adjust-
> ments you can follow God in obedience. Keep in
> mind—the God who calls you is also the One who
> will enable you to do His will.[3]

As we seek to possess God's wisdom, we will be able to move beyond simply expressing the vision and values of leaders. We

will possess the kind of character from which lofty visions and
values flow, the kind of character that isn't swayed by public
opinion or fear but pursues true greatness and knows who the
real audience is. Our character will be truly godly, so that others
will delight in following us.

GOD: HE'S QUITE A CHARACTER!

Think about the people you know and admire. Do you
know any wise mothers and fathers who demonstrate
sound judgment in the way they conduct their lives and raise
their children? Do you know any grandparents who know
when to cheer and when to rebuke, when to be tender and
when to use force? Have you ever had a teacher who knew
when to give advice and when to just listen, when to instruct
and when to let life's consequences be the instructor? Now try
to put a value on those wise insights. How much are they
worth?

We all esteem people who possess wisdom in their inward
character. If we admire these high-quality people, how much
more should we value the perfection of the living God from
whom all wisdom, patience, and discernment are derived?

When Moses asked God to reveal his glory to him, the Lord
said, "I will cause all my goodness to pass in front of you, and I
will proclaim my name, the LORD, in your presence" (Exodus
33:18–19). God had to shield Moses from the fullness of his
glory by covering him in the cleft of a rock; and as he passed in
front of Moses, God accompanied this awesome display by pro-
claiming the perfection of his own character:

> And he passed in front of Moses, proclaiming, "The
> LORD, the LORD, the compassionate and gracious God,
> slow to anger, abounding in love and faithfulness,
> maintaining love to thousands, and forgiving wicked-
> ness, rebellion and sin. Yet he does not leave the

guilty unpunished; he punishes the children and
their children for the sin of the fathers to the third
and fourth generation." (Exodus 34:6–7)

When God revealed himself as the compassionate and gracious God who is slow to anger, who abounds in love and faithfulness, who maintains love to thousands, and who forgives wickedness, rebellion and sin, he made it clear that his personal character is the absolute standard by which all of these qualities are defined. God is accountable to no one, and there is no higher standard to which he must conform. As the great thinker Anselm said in the eleventh century, "God is that than which nothing greater can be conceived."

Anselm originally made this statement in an attempt to prove God's existence. But as Michael Witmer points out,

> The real legacy of Anselm's argument is not its
> attempt to prove God's existence but rather how it
> teaches us to speak about God. If God is "that than
> which nothing greater can be conceived," then we
> know there are certain things we must say about
> him. For starters, we must use only our best words to
> describe him. God must be righteous, powerful, loving, and kind—all the things that it is better to be
> than not to be. We may disagree about what items
> should go in the list ... but we all agree that the list
> must include all the great-making properties we can
> imagine....
>   God is qualitatively superior to anything in his
> creation. There is nothing that compares with the
> greatest possible being. He is in a class by himself—
> literally.[4]

God's own eternal and uncompromising character is the unchanging standard that gives ultimate meaning to love, graciousness, faithfulness, and forbearance. And yet the incredible call of the gospel is that fallen creatures such as we can now begin to reflect our heavenly Father's character in our own lives. The One who is goodness in his essence, the One who defines virtue by his very being, promises to empower those of us who will trust him enough to live according to his will.

CHARACTER FROM THE INSIDE OUT

People are not impressed by facades or manipulation, but by authenticity and by those who are genuinely others-centered. Character is not a matter of outward technique but of inner reality. God is concerned with what we are really like when no one else is looking. Douglas Rumford, in discussing the sad situation of a Christian leader who lost his ministry due to sexual misconduct, explains that this kind of thing is bound to happen when we allow a "character gap" to develop in our lives. He writes,

> The character gap is a weakness that will one day
> become apparent, when the circumstances or stresses
> of life converge and reach a breaking point. We may
> be able to coast for a while, and we may feel quite
> secure. But raw talent, personality, and fortunate cir-
> cumstances cannot substitute for the forging of inner
> holiness, resilience, and the convictions that comprise
> integrity of character.[5]

In 2 Peter 1:5–8 the apostle listed the qualities of life and godliness that God wants for each of his children:

> For this very reason, make every effort to add to
> your faith goodness; and to goodness, knowledge;
> and to knowledge, self-control; and to self-control,
> perseverance; and to perseverance, godliness; and to
> godliness, brotherly kindness; and to brotherly kind-
> ness, love. For if you possess these qualities in

increasing measure, they will keep you from being ineffective and unproductive in your knowledge of our Lord Jesus Christ.

The character qualities listed in these verses are admirable, but they are also overwhelming. We may aspire to these characteristics, but is it really possible for us to attain them? The answer, both from Scripture and from sheer human experience, is a resounding "No!" In our own strength, this kind of character is not merely difficult to attain; it is impossible to attain.

If it were simply a matter of fitful human effort, the attempt would be futile. So what are we to do? Shall we simply throw up our hands and walk away from the text, claiming that it makes impossible demands? That would be foolish. What we should do is pay attention to the context in which Peter wrote those words.

The sentences just prior to this passage (2 Peter 1:3–4) provide the necessary key: In Christ we have been permitted to access God's divine power and have been granted the incomprehensible privilege of participating "in the divine nature" (v. 4). There is only one person who is able to live the Christlike life: Jesus Christ himself. Without him, we cannot live the life he calls us to live (John 15:5). Only as we maintain our connection to him can he live this life through us. As Martin Luther said, "It is not imitation which brings about our sonship of God, but our sonship which makes possible imitation."[6] Not only have we received a new nature in Christ (Romans 6:6–13), we have also become indwelled by the Holy Spirit, whose power within us makes it possible for us to manifest these qualities of Christlike character.

True spiritual and character transformation takes place from the inside out, not from the outside in. The attributes of faith, goodness, knowledge, self-control, perseverance, godliness, brotherly kindness, and love flow from the life of Christ that has been implanted within us.

PETER: A CASE STUDY IN CHARACTER

It is easy to read Peter's inspirational words and wonder, "Who thinks up this stuff? Where do people with such ideals and insights come from?" Well, the man who wrote those inspiring words, the man who exhorted us on to such strength of character, didn't always live up to those same ideals.

The man who called himself "a witness of Christ's sufferings" (1 Peter 5:1) was not there when Jesus was hanging on the cross; along with most of the other disciples he was hiding in fear (Matthew 26:69–75). The man who calls us to be "eager to serve" (1 Peter 5:2) remained seated while Jesus washed the disciples' feet, including his (John 13:1–10). The man who tells us that we should "be clear minded and self-controlled so that you can pray" (1 Peter 4:7) fell asleep while Jesus was in such intense prayer that his sweat was like drops of blood (Luke 22:39–46). The man who so boldly tells us to "submit yourselves for the Lord's sake to every authority instituted among men" (1 Peter 2:13) took a sword and lopped off the ear of an official from the chief priests and Pharisees (John 18:10–11).

None of this examination of the startling difference between his words and his actions is meant to demean Peter. The point here is to give us hope. This man Peter, who was so impulsive and immature, grew into a great leader of the church. The Peter we read about in the four Gospels became the Peter we read about in the book of Acts and the Peter who wrote two epistles. It took time and effort, but God transformed him. And the same Holy Spirit who worked this transformation in Peter's life is actively at work transforming those of us who have placed our faith in his Son Jesus Christ.

The Gospels leave us with two impressions of Peter. The first is that he was at times a comically impulsive character. Twice he jumped out of perfectly seaworthy boats, fully clothed. He challenged Jesus; he spoke out of turn; at times, he seemed to demonstrate more energy and creativity than was appropriate for the moment. But it is that very energy and creativity that underlie the second impression of Peter.

Peter was the disciples' unofficial leader. He often served as their spokesperson. Along with James and John, he was one of the three disciples in Jesus' "inner circle." Certainly after Jesus' departure, the disciples looked to Peter to give them direction. Luke's record of the church's early years (the book of Acts) leaves no doubt about Peter's leadership.

This seemingly conflicting combination of qualities exists in many young leaders and may be identified by a term such as "high mental energy." Peter was always thinking, and he always thought with a view toward action. When he heard "question," he immediately thought "answer." When he observed "problem," he thought "solution." When he encountered "options," he thought "decision." But he also demonstrated the unfortunate side of that same characteristic. When he heard "silence," he thought "talk." When he encountered "disagreement," he thought "challenge." "Error" (or at least Peter's perception of error) sparked "correction." But whatever the situation, at the very least he *did* think, and his thinking inevitably led to action.

In his younger years Peter exercised little constraint, and his answers, solutions, decisions, and speech sometimes seemed buffoonish. At times his behavior was perceived as insensitive, unconsidered, and immature. But like many great leaders, Peter survived himself. With Jesus' guidance, Peter's fertile and active mind matured. Through all of his experiences he developed a more godly, Christlike character. This maturity led his thinking process into more productive channels. He collected, collated, and connected information. He honed his reasoning skills. Peter became a leader because he was not afraid to make a decision. And his godly character informed the decisions he made.

Anyone serving under a leader who suffers "paralysis by analysis" will appreciate Peter's quick response time. Anyone working in an organization in which "decision by indecision" is the rule understands why people were drawn to Peter. As we follow Peter's life through the Gospels and then hear his mature voice resonate throughout his two epistles, we appreciate this optimistic, energetic, highly intelligent man of action and deep character. In fact, the gospel of Mark, which many believe Peter dictated to Mark, is the gospel that portrays Jesus as a man of action and urgency. The Greek word translated *immediately* is used forty-two times in Mark's sixteen chapters.

When the church was on the move, when both the Roman and Jewish leaders were opposing it, when Christians were being martyred for their faith, someone needed to make quick, Spirit-led decisions. And we can only imagine the kinds of issues that could have splintered this frail organization when the church leaped over its cultural boundaries to include Greek-speaking Jews, then Samaritans, then local Gentiles, then Asians and Greeks and Romans. Because Peter was a leader whose ego could endure the threat of disagreement, challenge, or even a bad decision, he was not afraid to act. He was not careless, nor did he deal frivolously with critical matters. His godly character wouldn't allow him to do so. But he was not afraid to move, and under his leadership the church got things done. Peter was a leader who made decisions that mattered.

Loving Our Way to Good Character

It is amazing what God can do with people who want to grow personally and develop character. The great news is that God wants us to grow as much as we can. He redeemed us for that purpose. To discover the lengths to which God will go to forge steel into our characters, let's walk through the smelting furnace along with Peter.

This man had denied Jesus at a critical time; yet later in his life he suffered beatings, imprisonment, and eventually death rather than deny him again. We all know that such character is not developed in a single event. We know that Jesus' resurrection had a profound influence on Peter's character transformation. But the manner in which Jesus helped Peter to recover from the worst failure of his life should afford us great encouragement about asking the same Lord Jesus to help us to develop strength of character as well.

> Now Peter was sitting out in the courtyard, and a servant girl came to him. "You also were with Jesus of Galilee," she said.
> But he denied it before them all. "I don't know what you're talking about," he said.
> Then he went out to the gateway, where another girl saw him and said to the people there, "This fellow was with Jesus of Nazareth."
> He denied it again, with an oath: "I don't know the man!"
> After a little while, those standing there went up to Peter and said, "Surely you are one of them, for your accent gives you away."
> Then he began to call down curses on himself and he swore to them, "I don't know the man!"
> Immediately a rooster crowed. Then Peter remembered the word Jesus had spoken: "Before the rooster crows, you will disown me three times." And he went outside and wept bitterly. (Matthew 26:69–75)

To discover just what this event represented to Peter, perhaps we should go back and read a passage from earlier in the same chapter:

> Then Jesus told them, "This very night you will all fall away on account of me...."
> Peter replied, "Even if all fall away on account of you, I never will."
> "I tell you the truth," Jesus answered, "this very night, before the rooster crows, you will disown me three times."
> But Peter declared, "Even if I have to die with

you, I will never disown you." And all the other disciples said the same. (Matthew 26:31, 33–35)

At this earlier point, Peter's strength of character could
hardly be questioned. He said he was willing to die with Jesus if
he had to. But the Son of God was right. That same night, Peter
denied even knowing Jesus.

Following all of these events, Jesus was crucified and buried.
Three days later he was raised from the dead and was seen
briefly by the disciples (John 20). But the first conversation
between Jesus and Peter, recorded in John 21, shows how Jesus
dealt with Peter's failure:

> When they had finished eating, Jesus said to Simon
> Peter, "Simon son of John, do you truly love me
> more than these?"
> "Yes, Lord," he said, "you know that I love you."
> Jesus said, "Feed my lambs."
> Again Jesus said, "Simon son of John, do you
> truly love me?"
> He answered, "Yes, Lord, you know that I love
> you."
> Jesus said, "Take care of my sheep."
> The third time he said to him, "Simon son of
> John, do you love me?"
> Peter was hurt because Jesus asked him the third
> time, "Do you love me?" He said, "Lord, you know
> all things; you know that I love you."
> Jesus said, "Feed my sheep." (John 21:15–18)

Notice Peter's sound theological affirmation in verse 17:
"Lord, you know all things; you know that I love you." Peter
was correct. Jesus wasn't asking Peter the question because *he*
needed to know that answer but because *Peter* needed to know
that answer. Why was it so important for Peter to come to grips
with his own answer to that question? It is important for us as
well to determine whether our love for Jesus Christ is strong

enough to enable us to develop the character qualities his Word encourages and demands. These are the qualities Peter listed in 2 Peter 1:5–8.

In the first twelve chapters of the book of Acts we see Peter as the prominent leader in the fledgling church. His strength of character and conviction are a source of inspiration, challenge, and encouragement to many. Our Lord is still seeking men and women who will answer, "Yes, Lord, you know that I love you," and who will then develop the character qualities needed to be godly leaders.

FORGING CHARACTER

Character is forged in the small things of life. The big events of life can be viewed as final examinations that reveal the true nature of our inward selves. It is in the seemingly unimportant decisions that our character is strengthened bit by bit. C. S. Lewis used the image of the "central core" within each of us that is formed and molded by our choices:

> People often think of Christian morality as a kind of
> bargain in which God says, "If you keep a lot of rules
> I'll reward you, and if you don't I'll do the other
> thing." I do not think that is the best way of looking
> at it. I would much rather say that every time you
> make a choice you are turning the central part of
> you, the part of you that chooses, into something a
> little different from what it was before. And taking
> your life as a whole, with all your innumerable
> choices, all your life long you are slowly turning this
> central thing either into a heavenly creature or a
> hellish creature: either into a creature that is in har-
> mony with God and with other creatures, and with
> itself, or else into one that is in a state of war and
> hatred with God, and with its fellow-creatures, and
> with itself. To be the one kind of creature is heaven:

that is, it is joy and peace and knowledge and power. To be the other means madness, horror, idiocy, rage, impotence, and eternal loneliness. Each of us at each moment is progressing to the one state or the other.[7]

The choices we make today determine our character. And we will take our characters with us into eternity. Therefore, we must choose wisely!

1. Marjorie J. Thompson, *Soul Feast: An Invitation to the Christian Spiritual Life* (Louisville, KY: Westminster John Knox, 1995), 11.
2. Douglas J. Rumford, *Soul Shaping: Taking Care of Your Spiritual Life* (Wheaton, IL: Tyndale, 1996), 354.
3. Henry T. Blackaby and Claude V. King, *Experiencing God* (Nashville: Broadman & Holman, 1994), 147, 151, 153.
4. Michael E. Witmer, *Heaven Is a Place on Earth* (Grand Rapids, MI: Zondervan, 2004), 40.
5. Rumford, *Soul Shaping*, 354.
6. Quoted in Gordon S. Wakefield, *The Westminster Dictionary of Christian Spirituality* (Philadelphia: Westminster Press, 1983), 209.
7. C. S. Lewis, *Mere Christianity* (New York: Macmillan, 1943), 86–87.

CHAPTER 3

Values

THE IMPORTANCE OF CONSISTENT VALUES

Values are essential to effective leadership. They are the uncompromisable, undebatable truths that drive and direct our behavior. They are motivational, explaining to us *why* we do things; and they are restrictive, placing boundaries around our behavior. Values are those things that we deem important and that provide direction and guidance in spite of our emotions.

Authors writing on the subject of leadership are paying increased attention to the importance of consistent values to a leader's effectiveness over the long haul.[1] Businesses, political and educational organizations, churches, families, and individuals all benefit from knowing and living by their core values. In business, core values are "the organization's essential and enduring tenets—a small set of general guiding principles; not to be confused with specific cultural or operating practices; not to be compromised for financial gain or short-term expediency."[2] Jim Collins and Jerry Porras observe that all enduring visionary companies have a set of core values that determine the behavior of the group.[3]

King David described value-driven behavior in Psalm 15:1–5:

LORD, who may dwell in your sanctuary? Who may
live on your holy hill?

He whose walk is blameless and who does what
is righteous, who speaks the truth from his heart and
has no slander on his tongue, who does his neighbor
no wrong and casts no slur on his fellowman, who
despises a vile man but honors those who fear the
LORD, who keeps his oath even when it hurts, who
lends his money without usury and does not accept a
bribe against the innocent.

He who does these things will never be shaken.

Notice that David said that the person who enjoys the presence of God and lives a blameless life is the one who "speaks
the truth from his heart" (v. 2). Because this person values
truth in his heart, his words express truth. Because he values
kindness, he "does his neighbor no wrong" (v. 3). Because he
values honesty, he "keeps his oath even when it hurts" (v. 4).
Because he values justice, he "does not accept a bribe against
the innocent" (v. 5).

Leaders who are driven by values reap a great benefit from
the Lord. David said they "will never be shaken" (v. 5).
Regardless of what may happen around them, they can live with
full confidence that the right principles have shaped their values
and have guided their decisions. That confidence will give them
emotional and spiritual stability. It will enable them to be leaders whom God can use for his glory.

Consider what values drove the behavior of the person
described by the psalmist. As you examine your own life, what
values do you see as driving your behavior? Many of us hold
certain values, but our actions are not governed by the things
we say we hold dear. Perhaps we should start by asking ourselves what values we *want* to have driving our behavior. Unless
we become intentional about doing so, we will be shaped by the
values of others. We cannot have a set of values for the office,
another set for the home, and a completely different set for

church activities. Our goal should be to completely integrate godly values into *all* spheres of our daily life.

GOD: THE SOURCE OF ALL VALUES

God is accountable to no one, and there is no higher authority to which he must conform. He himself is the absolute of truth, beauty, goodness, love, and justice. His perfect character is the essence of what the Bible calls "righteousness." In a universe without God, what we call "good" would have no ultimate referent.

God's moral structures and values are built into the created order. The Bible affirms that even those who have not been exposed to God's law have a conscience—a moral law—within them (Romans 2:14–16). God is revealed not only in nature, but also in the human heart. Our hearts and consciences reveal the fingerprints of a moral God. C. S. Lewis used the idea of an omnipresent, self-evident law as the starting point for his classic, *Mere Christianity*, what he called the Law of Nature or the Moral Law. A few years later, in *The Abolition of Man*, he simply called it the Tao that is in all cultures and societies. There is a surprisingly uniform moral absolute in most cultures—Babylonian, Egyptian, Persian, Chinese. None of these, for example, honors treachery or selfishness, cowardice or deceit. These standards are there because God has placed his natural law, his moral law, in human hearts. Try as we might, we simply cannot deny it.

Lewis also said, "Unless we allow ultimate reality to be moral, we cannot morally condemn it."[4] By that, he meant that unless there is some agreed-upon standard for the true, the beautiful, and the good, there can be no absolute standard by which to condemn "evil" behavior. In other words, people who use the presence of evil and suffering to denounce God are really appealing to God to condemn God. In fact, when people talk about evil in this world, they imply the existence of the God of the Bible, because if there is no God, then the idea of evil is arbitrary. One man's meat is another man's poison, so to speak. Even our notions of good and evil come to us because we bear the image of the One who initially determined the categories.

If our world continues to denounce the idea of moral absolutes, it cannot also continue to denounce the misappropriation of power and the misconduct of rich and powerful people. In a world that fails to acknowledge God as the final absolute, self-serving pragmatism will rule. The fact that people are seduced by power and wealth should not be surprising; what should surprise us is that such seduction is not more widespread than it already is. Christian counselor Larry Hall says:

> As long as our morality continues to be based in our humanistic pride, moral consistency will elude us. We will go on being bundles of self-contradiction, wildly judging each other while vehemently demanding that no one judge us. We can forget about arriving at a consensus ethic. There is virtually no consensus in a society as pluralistic as ours. About the most we can hope for is some sense of political correctness, and who in their right mind would hope for that? Even if true consensus were possible, history has proven repeatedly that such a consensus can be very immoral. When ethics are based on self and pride, all objectivity is lost. Things are no longer right or wrong. Instead, they are feasible or impractical, desirable or unappealing, agreeable or nonnegotiable…. Indeed, the very concepts of virtue and vice become meaningless.[5]

Godly Values for Godly People

As human beings, the crown of God's creation, we should be aware that God has "set eternity in the hearts of [people]" (Ecclesiastes 3:11). As godly leaders, we should seek to live by God's eternal values of truth, beauty, goodness, love, and justice set forth in the biblical record. If we look to the world for our moral values, we will be confused by self-interest, social conditioning, and situational ethics. The values of our culture are shallow and subjective, but the moral standards of Scripture reflect God's absolute and unchanging character. Exodus 20:1–17 provides us the clearest summary of God's values for his people:

> And God spoke all these words:
> "I am the LORD your God, who brought you out of Egypt, out of the land of slavery.
> "You shall have no other gods before me.
> "You shall not make for yourself an idol in the form of anything in heaven above or on the earth beneath or in the waters below. You shall not bow down to them or worship them; for I, the LORD your God, am a jealous God, punishing the children for the sin of the fathers to the third and fourth generation of those who hate me, but showing love to a thousand generations of those who love me and keep my commandments.
> "You shall not misuse the name of the LORD your God, for the LORD will not hold anyone guiltless who misuses his name.
> "Remember the Sabbath day by keeping it holy. Six days you shall labor and do all your work, but the seventh day is a Sabbath to the LORD your God. On it you shall not do any work, neither you, nor your son or daughter, nor your manservant or maidservant, nor your animals, nor the alien within your gates. For in six days the LORD made the heavens and the earth, the sea, and all that is in them, but he rested on the seventh day. Therefore the LORD blessed the Sabbath day and made it holy.
> "Honor your father and your mother, so that you may live long in the land the LORD your God is giving you.

"You shall not murder.

"You shall not commit adultery.

"You shall not steal.

"You shall not give false testimony against your neighbor.

"You shall not covet your neighbor's house. You shall not covet your neighbor's wife, or his manservant or maidservant, his ox or donkey, or anything that belongs to your neighbor."

God's moral law for his people is an expression of his own changeless perfection. In the Ten Commandments, God is actually calling his covenant people to be like him. "I am the LORD who brought you up out of Egypt to be your God; therefore be holy, because I am holy" (Leviticus 11:45).

The Ten Commandments begin with a demonstrated relationship with God and end with relationships with others. In Scripture, righteousness is always realized within the context of relationships; it consistently relates to loving behavior toward God and others. "Love does no harm to its neighbor" (Romans 13:10). "The entire law is summed up in a single command: 'Love your neighbor as yourself'" (Galatians 5:14).

MOVING FROM THEORY TO PRACTICE

It is one thing to know the right things to do and another to consistently do them. Jesus called us to be perfect as our heavenly Father is perfect (Matthew 5:48), but this is unattainable apart from the power of the indwelling Holy Spirit. Larry Hall asserts, "Indeed, achieving transcendent virtue while denying transcendence is as absurdly impossible as grabbing my own collar and lifting myself off the ground."[6] Only as we live by the Spirit are we empowered to incarnate biblical values and make them real in our own lives. Values are interesting to discuss in the abstract, but sometimes "values" get in the way of valuable decisions. Maintaining his values can cost a leader dearly. So how do we decide what matters most when we are weighing the bottom-line costs against our bottom-line convictions?

The first step in effective leadership is defining core values. Until that is done, the ship the leader is trying to steer has no rudder. Vision, mission, strategy, and outcome are difficult—if not impossible—to define until values are clear. Jesus knew that truth. Early in the process of developing his team of disciples, he forced them to confront this foundational issue.

Jesus' primer on values is recorded in Matthew 6:1–34. Jesus focused his lesson in verses 19–21:

> Do not store up for yourselves treasures on earth, where moth and rust destroy, and where thieves break in and steal. But store up for yourselves treasures in heaven, where moth and rust do not destroy, and where thieves do not break in and steal. For where your treasure is, there your heart will be also.

Jesus urged his disciples to focus their values on things that would bear an eternal return. But how, while making a living, responsibly leading an enterprise, and providing jobs, product, service, and profit on earth, do we build treasure in heaven? This passage presents the crux of the value question. Jesus begins this portion of the Sermon on the Mount by saying, "Be careful not to do your 'acts of righteousness' before men, to be seen by them. If you do, you will have no reward from your Father in heaven" (Matthew 6:1). That is the idea: For whom do we really work? Whose nod of approval is most important to us? Who defines what really matters in our lives?

In essence, Jesus was telling his disciples—and us—that the core value, the driving value, the eternal value, is summed up in this one question: "Does what I am doing please God?" Every other value is second to that one. When that value is in place, all other values line up. Matthew 6 is among the most definitive chapters in the Bible for shaping our philosophy of life and leadership. Spending time meditating on Jesus' words here will have inestimable value in our role as leaders.

PAUL WRESTLED WITH TWO ALTERNATIVES

Often the temptation is to rationalize our lives in such a way that no matter what we do, we can convince ourselves that it's okay. It's like the story about the FBI being called into a small town to investigate the work of what appeared to be a sharpshooter. They were amazed to find bull's-eyes drawn all over town, with bullets that had penetrated the exact center of the targets. When they finally found the man who had been doing the shooting, they asked him how he had been able to shoot with such accuracy. His answer was simple: First he shot the bullet, then he drew the bull's-eye around the spot where it had hit.[7] Although it is fortunate that this "sharpshooter" had not caused any real damage with his errant shots, God is not honored by such a haphazard approach to living. He has called us to live our lives with precision and clarity of focus.

The apostle Paul wrestled with two desires. When he traced these desires back to their core values, he found a resolution:

> For to me, to live is Christ and to die is gain. If I am
> to go on living in the body, this will mean fruitful
> labor for me. Yet what shall I choose? I do not know!
> I am torn between the two: I desire to depart and be
> with Christ, which is better by far; but it is more nec-
> essary for you that I remain in the body. (Philippians
> 1:21–24)

Interestingly, Paul had a proper philosophy of death, and it gave rise to his proper philosophy of life. He, like Jesus, knew where he was going (cf. John 13:1). Once he knew his ultimate destination, he was free to understand who and what he was living for. Our lives are valuable only in light of our ultimate destiny. These brief and ephemeral years can be leveraged into eternity. So, Paul, writing from prison, understood that he couldn't really lose in his situation. Whether he was executed or acquitted, he won.

It was with this frame of mind that he wrote: "Convinced of this [the fact that my continued presence on earth is for your sake], I know that I will remain, and I will continue with all of you for your progress and joy in the faith, so that through my being with you again your joy in Christ Jesus will overflow on account of me" (Philippians 1:25–26). Once he was able to link his desires with his values, he possessed tremendous resolve.

Most leaders today also face the tension between competing value systems and structures. In the face of difficult daily decisions, the task of sorting out primary from secondary values can be frustrating. Hackman and Johnson, in their book *Leadership*, give us some further definition that may help in this dilemma. First they discuss what values are:

> Values are at the core of individual, group or organizational identity. Values are relatively enduring conceptions or judgments about what we consider to be important. [Substantial research suggests] that a number of positive effects result from agreement between personal values and the values most prized in the organization at which we work. Agreement between personal and organizational values results in increased personal identification with the organization, higher levels of job satisfaction, greater team effectiveness and lower turnover rates.[8]

Then these two authors go on to identify two types of values: "terminal values"—those that deal with lifelong goals; and "instrumental values"—those that govern behaviors that achieve terminal values. Among their list of eighteen terminal values are freedom, self-respect, mature love, family security, true friendship, wisdom, equality, and salvation. Some of the eighteen instrumental values they outline are being loving, independent, capable, broad-minded, honest, responsible, ambitious, forgiving, self-controlled, and courageous.

Paul began the passage in Philippians 1 above with a short vision statement: "For to me, to live is Christ and to die is gain" (v. 21). We could all do with writing a short vision statement for our own lives. This can be accomplished fairly easily. Simply add your personal values to both of the lists above, then rank the values in order of their importance to you. The authors then suggest that you "carefully examine the list of your top-rated terminal and instrumental values. Look for similarities, patterns, and themes."[9] Finally, forge a short vision statement from what you find by clarifying your values in this manner.

Paul wrestled with his desires until he clarified what he valued. Hackman and Johnson support Paul's decision-making process by telling us that people work better with clearly understood values. Leaders who want to be effective will find that clarifying and communicating values is an essential task. Ordering our terminal and instrumental values by rank of importance and forming a short vision statement will help us avoid taking a scattershot approach to living.

LIVING IN THE LAND OF OUR SOJOURN

We are all mortal. None of us knows how many days we have on this earth. In fact, this is one of the most common themes in Scripture—that of the pilgrim, the stranger, the sojourner. The late singer-songwriter Rich Mullins understood this imagery. His lyrics frequently made mention of a "longing for home" that sometimes caused him to weep. In the song "Land of My Sojourn," he wrote:

> Nobody tells you when you get born here
> How much you'll come to love it

And how you'll never belong here.
So I call you my country,
And I'll be lonely for my home.
I wish that I could take you there with me.[10]

We do not belong here on earth. This is merely a land we travel through on our way to our final destination. Our citizenship is in heaven. Thus our ultimate aspirations must transcend anything this world can provide. There are pleasant moments, to be sure, but there are also painful moments. We must change our thinking so that we can affirm, with the apostle Paul, that neither our temporary pleasures nor our present sufferings are "worth comparing with the glory that will be revealed in us" (Romans 8:18). These things are merely preparing us for what is to come.

As we grow and mature in the things of God, we can come to the place where our longing for our true home governs the way we live here in our temporary home. It is possible to endure great hardships and trials when we know that they are only temporary and are leading us to something far greater. Also, it is in this way that we come to see how precious our time here is, and how foolish it is to waste our time here with our noses to the grindstone or endlessly channel surfing! How terrible it would be to come to the end of life and realize that we had been too busy or preoccupied to actually live. While we are here we have opportunities to cultivate relationships and catalog experiences and share the gospel and serve people in need. Our boredom surely reveals more about us than about the God who places so many wonderful opportunities in our paths.

The central issue of values is summed up in what Jesus called the first and greatest commandment: "Love the Lord your God with all your heart and with all your soul and with all your mind" (Matthew 22:37). That is the value to value. That is the prism through which all other values must shine, the filter through which all of life's choices are made and solutions are drawn. Until we have learned to love God properly, the rest of what we have learned about values will remain an academic exercise.

1. For example, the following books have been released as of this date: *Executive Values: A Christian Approach to Organizational Leadership* by Kurt Senske (Augsburg Fortress Publishers); *Transformational Leadership: Value Based Management for Indian Organizations* by Shivganesh Bhargava (Sage Publications); *And Dignity for All: Unlocking Greatness with Values-Based Leadership* by James E. Despain, et al. (Financial Times Prentice Hall); *Living Headship: Voices, Values and Vision* by Helen M. Gunter, et al. (Paul Chapman Publications).
2. James C. Collins and Jerry I. Porras, *Built to Last* (New York: HarperBusiness, 1997), 73.
3. Ibid., 94.
4. C. S. Lewis, "De Futilitate," in *Christian Reflections* (Grand Rapids, MI: Eerdmans, 1967), 69.
5. Larry E. Hall, *No Longer I* (Abilene, TX: ACU Press, 1998), 126.
6. Ibid., 127.
7. Adapted from James Emery White, *Rethinking the Church* (Grand Rapids, MI: Baker, 1997), 33.
8. Michael Hackman and Craig Johnson, *Leadership: A Communication Perspective*, 2nd ed. (Prospect Heights, IL: Waveland Press, 1996), 89.
9. Ibid.
10. Rich Mullins, "Land of My Sojourn," *A Liturgy, a Legacy, and a Ragamuffin Band,* 1993, Reunion Records.

CHAPTER 4

Purpose and Passion

YOU CAN'T MISS IT!

"Just turn right after the railroad tracks. You can't miss it."
Locals have a quaint way of giving directions to lost motorists.
They make a lot of assumptions. "Go past the Johnson's old farm
to where the grocery store used to be." They forget about the
fork in the road or the new traffic signal. "You can't miss it,"
they insist. But the problem is that while *they* may not be able to
miss it, *we* often do. And, after traveling fifteen or twenty miles
out of our way, we have to turn around, go back to that last
intersection, and ask for directions again.

Sometimes we move through life thinking we can't miss it.
The next turn will be so obvious. There can't be any doubt about
which way to go at the next junction. But how many times have
we discovered, to our chagrin, that we are completely lost and
should have taken the other fork twenty miles back?

There is an old story about a commercial airline pilot who
came over the public-address system and said: "Ladies and gen-
tlemen, I have some good news and some bad news. The good
news is that we have a very strong tailwind and are making
excellent time. The bad news is that our navigation equipment
has gone down, so we have no idea where we are." Perhaps this
is a fitting analogy for many of us. We are making great time on

a road to nowhere. We are on the fast track, but we don't really
know where all of this is leading us. When we finally get where
we have been heading all these years, we discover that it wasn't
really where we wanted to be after all. So, we hop on another
treadmill, but it leads to the same disillusionment. How far do
we have to travel before we turn around, go back to that last
intersection, and ask for directions again?

A well-known poem by Thomas S. Jones Jr. says it like this:

> Across the fields of yesterday,
> He sometimes comes to me,
> A little lad just back from play—
> The lad I used to be.
>
> And yet he smiles so wistfully
> Once he has crept within,
> I wonder if he hopes to see
> The man I might have been.[1]

It is interesting to go back to the days of idealistic youth and
recall the things we hoped for, the kind of person we thought
we might become. But such nostalgic recollections can be
depressing. We wonder where the years have gone and what
happened to all our youthful dreams and goals. Could it be that
we took the wrong turn somewhere along the line? Is it too late
to rectify an error in judgment?

As followers of Jesus, we say that the answer is "No! It's
never too late." We always have the opportunity of turning
back and getting on the right track. Our source of direction is
far greater than the people who say, "You can't miss it." There
is a source that can tell us what life is really about. Found in the
pages of Scripture, particularly the Wisdom Literature, are
directions not just to "live and learn" but to "learn and live."
The promise of skillful living is made to all those who will "listen to advice and accept instruction" (Proverbs 19:20). In his
"Owner's Manual," God has revealed truths about life; the Bible

is a guidebook of sorts, a blueprint to living, the foundation of a well-built life, and a road map through the maze of confusion that our days often resemble. There is purpose and meaning, clarity and fulfillment, in this life. But it is found only as we navigate by the wisdom contained in the Word of God.

THE GREAT PURPOSE OF A GREAT GOD

Does Scripture reveal God's intention when he created humans who bear his image? If so, how can we discover God's deep passion and participate in it? Before we get too deep into this subject, let us recognize that even if God did tell us explicitly why he does what he does, we still wouldn't understand.

In *A Little Book of Coincidence* geometer John Martineau reveals the exquisite orbital patterns of the planets and the mathematical relationships that govern them. Through the movement of the moon, Venus, Mars, and Mercury, it becomes clear that Earth is special in more ways than simply being the right distance from the sun.[2] From looking into the heavens we realize that we have no idea just how complex the designer of all this must be. Nothing in the universe is random.

So, it is no wonder that this magnificent designer should tell us: "'For my thoughts are not your thoughts, neither are your ways my ways,' declares the LORD. 'As the heavens are higher than the earth, so are my ways higher than your ways and my thoughts than your thoughts'" (Isaiah 55:8–9). One other Scripture to keep at the forefront of our thinking is 1 Corinthians 13:12: "Now we see but a poor reflection as in a mirror; then we shall see face to face. Now [we] know in part; then [we] shall know fully, even as [we are] fully known."

These passages highlight the huge knowledge gap between God's intentions and what we know of God's intentions. Basically, the difference between God and human beings is greater than that between angels and insects. We simply do not have the capacity to grasp God's ultimate purposes in creating and sustaining the cosmos. Scripture does, however, reveal fragments of God's purposes that relate to our lives in this world. One such fragment is found in the words of the apostle Paul recorded in Ephesians 3:2–11. Here we gain a perspective on the purpose and passion of the God of creation:

> Surely you have heard about the administration of God's grace that was given to me for you, that is, the mystery made known to me by revelation, as I have already written briefly. In reading this, then, you will be able to understand my insight into the mystery of Christ, which was not made known to men in other generations as it has now been revealed by the Spirit to God's holy apostles and prophets. This mystery is that through the gospel the Gentiles are heirs together with Israel, members together of one body, and sharers together in the promise in Christ Jesus.
>
> I became a servant of this gospel by the gift of God's grace given me through the working of his power. Although I am less than the least of all God's people, this grace was given me: to preach to the Gentiles the unsearchable riches of Christ, and to make plain to everyone the administration of this mystery, which for ages past was kept hidden in God, who created all things. His intent was that now, through the church, the manifold wisdom of God should be made known to the rulers and authorities in the heavenly realms, according to his eternal purpose which he accomplished in Christ Jesus our Lord.

God's eternal purposes reflect his perfect and eternal wisdom, and he has designed the world in such a way that we are most happy when he is glorified in our lives. For reasons that are incomprehensible to us, God has a passion for intimacy with his people, and we participate in his eternal purposes when we pursue him with undivided hearts.

Sometimes we just read over a statement like that last one and fail to be struck by just how profound and breathtaking it is: *God has a passion for intimacy with his people*. Singer-songwriter Michael Card put it in fundamental terms when he sang of God, "Could it be that You would really rather die than live without us?"[3] That is the length to which God will go in his pursuit of fellowship with us. His desire is more than mere words; it is so strong that it prompted him to enter into human history. The apostle John wrote, "This is love: not that we loved God, but that he loved us and sent his Son as an atoning sacrifice for our sins" (1 John 4:10). God believed intimate fellowship with us to be worth the death of his own Son. Who could possibly comprehend such love?

> You are beautiful beyond description,
> Too marvelous for words,
> Too wonderful for comprehension,
> Like nothing ever seen or heard.
> Who can grasp your infinite wisdom?
> Who can fathom the depth of your love?
> You are beautiful beyond description,
> Majesty enthroned in love.[4]

This is the God who wants to know us. This is the God who gave his Son as a ransom for us. The God who created billions and billions of stars, the God who arranged the heavens with the ease of an interior decorator hanging curtains, desires intimacy with us to the point that he was willing to enter our world with all its limitations and allow us to crucify him. If that is so, life can be truly meaningful only when we find that God glorified in our lives.

The obvious questions that beg to be asked are: "If a God could create and sustain a universe as amazingly complex as ours, if that same God could put together a plan to redeem lost and fallen humanity, if that God would go to such great lengths to rescue people who don't even know they are in peril, can that

God be trusted? Can it be that his purpose for our lives is better than that which we might construct on our own?" The answer is: "Of course!" But before we pat ourselves on the back for having answered correctly, the follow-up questions loom large: "So what? What are the implications of this belief? How are our lives to reflect it?"

Practice reveals priorities and beliefs. We can have a cognitive affirmation that God has a better purpose than anything we could come up with, but does it show in our practice? Contrary to public opinion, in releasing ourselves to God's purposes and giving ourselves wholeheartedly and unreservedly to him, we are not *sacrificing* anything other than the illusion of self-sufficiency. We are embracing something altogether wonderful.

Three Dimensions of God's Purpose for Us

While Scripture provides us only glimpses of God's *ultimate* purposes in creating the cosmos, the Word does reveal God's *universal* purpose for believers. In short, this purpose is to know Christ and to make him known. God does not want anyone to perish, but desires that everyone come to repentance and enter into a relationship with him through the new birth in Christ (2 Peter 3:9). Once a person is born again as a child of God, God wants that person to grow in Christ and be "conformed to the likeness of his Son" (Romans 8:29). Thus, God's purpose for each of us is edification (spiritual growth) and evangelism (spiritual reproduction).

God also has a *unique* purpose for each of us, and it relates to our distinctive temperaments, abilities, experiences, spiritual gifts, education, and spheres of influence. Why do we get out of bed in the morning? What is our life purpose? Few people can articulate a clear purpose statement for their lives. It is ironic that people tend to put more time and effort into planning a two-week vacation than they do in planning the final destination of their life's earthly journey. In Paul's second letter to the

church at Corinth we find more of an eternal perspective on this
temporal journey:

> Therefore we do not lose heart. Though outwardly
> we are wasting away, yet inwardly we are being
> renewed day by day. For our light and momentary
> troubles are achieving for us an eternal glory that far
> outweighs them all. So we fix our eyes not on what
> is seen, but on what is unseen. For what is seen is
> temporary, but what is unseen is eternal.
> (2 Corinthians 4:16–18)

This passage provides the context for God's unique purposes
for our lives, and reminds us to develop an eternal perspective
so that we will have a passion to give our lives in exchange for
the things that God tells us will endure.

GOD'S PROMISES BREED PASSION

What is it about some leaders? They seem to have that extra
"oomph!" Their followers are unusually productive, griev-
ances from their area are infrequent, and work quality is high.
People from other areas want to be transferred to their depart-
ments. What is their secret? Passion! Enthusiasm! These leaders
have a clearly defined purpose that transcends merely pushing
product out the door.

As godly leaders, our purpose in life needs to be directed
toward God and his kingdom. Does that mean that we are to
sit idly by and wait for Christ's return? No. In 2 Corinthians
5:9 the apostle Paul made it clear that we need to please God
both in this life and the next: "So we make it our goal to
please him, whether we are at home in the body or away
from it."

Paul knew that one day the Lord would replace his earthly
body with a resurrection body. While Paul didn't want to be

separated from his present body, he longed to be clothed with his new one. Such a longing didn't lead the apostle to try to escape life or to dismiss it as meaningless. On the contrary, that hope spurred him to try to please Christ. As followers of Christ our passion for the Savior both drives and defines our purpose for living. Brennan Manning, in his book *The Lion and the Lamb*, writes about two ways of discerning our passion and purpose. First, he advises us to recall what has saddened us recently. He asks:

> Was it the realization that you don't love Jesus enough, that you don't seek his face in prayer often enough, that you can't honestly say that the greatest thing that ever happened in your life is that he came to you and you heard his voice? Or have you been saddened and depressed over a lack of human respect, criticism from an authority figure, financial problems, lack of friends or your bulging waistline?[5]

Then he asks,

> What has gladdened you recently? Reflection on your election to the Christian community, the joy of praying, "Abba, I belong to you"? The afternoon you stole away with the gospel as your only companion, the filling awareness that God loves you unconditionally, just as you are and not as you should be? A small victory over selfishness? Or, were the sources of your gladness enjoying a new car, a suit, a movie and a pizza, a trip to Paris?[6]

By asking ourselves these questions we come face to face with what makes us tick as individuals. What are the primary motivations in our lives? Once we face these personal questions and answers spiritually, we can begin to take our personal passion and purpose and apply it organizationally.

In his book *The Purpose-Driven Church*, Rick Warren articulates the importance of translating our purpose into practical strategies. Among other things, he suggests the following:

- Program around your purposes. Design a program to fulfill each of your purposes.
- Educate your people on purpose. Change doesn't happen by chance; it occurs as you cultivate settings and procedures that facilitate the education of those you serve.
- Start small groups on purpose. Rather than forcing everyone to conform to a "one size fits all" mentality, urge your people to choose the type of small group that best fits their needs.
- Add staff on purpose. Rather than just hiring people who possess character and competence, look for staff with a passion for the purpose of the church. People are self-motivated about an area in which they have passion.
- Structure on purpose. Develop structures or teams that work together to systematically fulfill the purpose of the church.
- Evaluate on purpose. Consistent effectiveness in an ever-changing world requires continual evaluation. Remember that "in a purpose-driven church, your purposes are the standard by which you evaluate effectiveness."
- In leadership circles these days there is a lot of talk about vision, and rightly so. However, much of the organizational malaise found in companies, churches, and families is not caused by a lack of vision but by a lack of strategy. If we fail to strategize according to an overarching purpose, we will never accomplish the things God wants for us.[7]

The overall purpose of our lives must match up with his agenda. Otherwise, we will live out our lives in frustration and futility. God has structured reality so that when he is honored first and foremost, satisfaction comes as a by-product. May he grant us the courage and grace to honor him in all our ways.

THE SECRET TO PAUL'S PRODUCTIVITY

The apostle Paul accomplished an astounding amount in two decades of ministry. What made him tick? What drove him to carry out the work that he did? We find the secret in his own words found in Philippians 3:7–9:

> But whatever was to my profit I now consider loss
> for the sake of Christ. What is more, I consider
> everything a loss compared to the surpassing great-
> ness of knowing Christ Jesus my Lord, for whose
> sake I have lost all things. I consider them rubbish,
> that I may gain Christ and be found in him, not hav-
> ing a righteousness of my own that comes from the
> law, but that which is through faith in Christ—the
> righteousness that comes from God and is by faith.

This passage explodes with Paul's passion for his calling. Effective leaders, like Paul, are those who have figured out what they stand for. They have identified their purpose and pursue it with a passion.

Before his dramatic conversion (Acts 9), Paul followed a different purpose in life. As a Pharisee, Paul had attained the highest levels of status. In this instance he could have boasted about his religious training, heritage, and practice. He had been, in every sense, a "Hebrew of Hebrews" (Philippians 3:5), and his credentials would have impressed the most devout Jew. He was a passionate man, but he was passionate about the wrong things. After his encounter with the risen Lord, Paul considered all he had attained through religious effort to be garbage when compared with the value of knowing Christ. Paul was more than happy to throw away all he had attained in order to know Christ. The greatest achievements of this world are fine. There is nothing inherently wrong with them. But in the eternal scheme of things, Paul said, they are rubbish. As he noted in Philippians 3:8, compared with the value of knowing Christ, they are trash. Actually the Greek word is *skubala*. It is a hard word to translate, and it is a word that makes a lot of church people uncomfortable. The *King James Version* renders it "dung," but even that is a mild form of what Paul is saying. Paul is using bumper-sticker language: *Skubala* happens! That's how he described the eternal value of our earthly accomplishments. Ultimately, our worth and purpose extends far beyond the temporal things we achieve in this life.

Paul preached that in Christ he and all believers possess all the righteousness of God. Because of our faith in Jesus and our identification with him, we can have peace with the one who created us, the one for whom we were made. Because of the infinite worth of knowing Christ, Paul devoted his life to knowing the Savior. That was his purpose and his passion. And that purpose and passion shaped all he did and influenced all those he led to the Lord.

This is not to say that our purpose eliminates all other concerns. Bills must still be paid; food and shelter do not miraculously fall from the sky. It is even legitimate for us to desire success in business and to have career aspirations. However, Benjamin Hunnicutt, a University of Iowa authority on the history of work, notes that work has become our new religion, where we worship and give our time and energy. As our commitment to family, community, and faith shrinks, we begin to look to our careers to provide us with meaning, identity, and esteem.[8] We must be ever watchful to keep our calling (something we do *for* God) from becoming a career (something that threatens to *become* god).

Compared with knowing Christ, our activities from eight to five Monday through Friday don't matter very much. In the end, what will matter is whether or not we know him, regardless of what else is on our résumés or in our portfolios. When we stand before God and hear him ask us, "Why should I let you into heaven?" what will we say? "I was a vice president in my company"? "I did well in the market"? "I was on the board of the country club"? "I was active in my church"? None of these answers is satisfactory. Only one will suffice: "Jesus forgave my sins and gave me his righteousness." In making that simple statement, our ultimate purpose can begin to become clear.

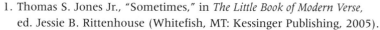

1. Thomas S. Jones Jr., "Sometimes," in *The Little Book of Modern Verse,* ed. Jessie B. Rittenhouse (Whitefish, MT: Kessinger Publishing, 2005).
2. John Martineau, *A Little Book of Coincidence* (New York: Walker & Company, 2002).
3. Michael Card, "Could It Be," *Present Reality,* 1981, Sparrow Records.
4. Mark Altrogge, "I Stand in Awe," 1987, *Worship Favorites from PDI Music,* PDI Praise.
5. Brennan Manning, *Lion and Lamb* (Grand Rapids, MI: Revell, 1986), 43.
6. Ibid.
7. Adapted from Rick Warren, *The Purpose-Driven Church* (Grand Rapids, MI: Zondervan, 1995), 137–52.
8. Benjamin Kline Hunnicutt, *Work Without End: Abandoning Shorter Hours for the Right to Work* (Philadelphia: Temple University Press, 1988).

CHAPTER 5

Humility

IT'S HARD TO BE HUMBLE

Woody Allen is credited with saying, "If you want to make God laugh, tell him your plans." We could add to it, "If you want to hear him laugh even louder, tell him how much you know." Just because these statements are true, however, doesn't make them easy to accept. It is hard to admit that we do not know as much as we think we know. And we certainly aren't in control of as much as we would like to think. We make our plans, but it is God who controls the outcome (Proverbs 16:9). We make our plans, but we understand that "if it is the Lord's will, we will live and do this or that" (James 4:15).

John Ruskin said: "I believe that the first test of a truly great man is his humility. I don't mean by humility, doubt of his power. But really great men have a curious feeling that the greatness is not of them, but through them. And they see something divine in every other man and are endlessly, foolishly, incredibly merciful."[1]

The modern notion of the "self-made" people pulling themselves up by their own bootstraps and, by the sweat of their own brow, climbing to the pinnacle of success is so deeply imbedded in our consciousness that any other possibility seems foreign. It is humbling to recognize that God is more responsible for the achievements of our lives than we are, that we are people who have been *given* our abilities, time, and opportunities. These things are not our possession; they are gifts from God, and we will ultimately give an account for what we do with what we have been given (cf. Matthew 25:14–30). Everything in us strains against this notion, for to accept it as fact is to be humbled.

Humility is such an elusive virtue. As soon as we think we have it, we don't. That's part of the problem: When we finally achieve humility, we get proud of ourselves. Our humility cries out for recognition. Humility is terribly fragile.

Part of the reason for this elusiveness is that humility has a difficult time coexisting with self-awareness. True humility comes when we are consumed with awareness of Another. According to Thomas Alexander Fyfe's book *Who's Who in Dickens*, Uriah Heep, one of Dickens' characters in *David Copperfield*, was "a hypocritical plotter who feigned humility; a swindler and forger who was ultimately exposed." He was fond of quoting his father, "Be 'umble, Uriah, says father to me, and you'll get on." Yet, at one point in the book he said to Master Copperfield, "Ah! But you know we're so very 'umble…. And having such a knowledge of our own 'umbleness, we must really take care that we're not pushed to the wall by them as isn't 'umble."[2]

Saying we are humble or thinking of ourselves as modest is actually a perverted form of pride. The key to humility is to get our eyes off ourselves and onto the One from whom and for whom and through whom all things are (cf. 1 Corinthians 8:6; Colossians 1:16–20).

The church in Philippi was experiencing some tension, and in his letter to them Paul stated that one of the keys to unity in the church is being focused on the same thing.

> If you have any encouragement from being united
> with Christ, if any comfort from his love, if any fel-
> lowship with the Spirit, if any tenderness and

compassion, then make my joy complete by being like-minded, having the same love, being one in spirit and purpose. Do nothing out of selfish ambition or vain conceit, but in humility consider others better than yourselves. Each of you should look not only to your own interests, but also to the interests of others. (Philippians 2:1–4)

To avoid disharmony in the body of Christ, we must all have "the same love"—Jesus Christ. The more we love Jesus, the more we are able to love one another. Then, and only then, can there exist a united sense of purpose. Then we can refrain from manipulation or self-serving actions. Then we can truly serve others selflessly.

THE HUMILITY OF GOD

Let us first examine the supreme biblical example of humility: the incarnate God who made himself known in our world. In Philippians 2, we learn about Christ's self-emptying servant nature. Here we find an important principle in Scripture: before honor comes humility. The cross comes before the crown; the person who seeks honor will ultimately be humiliated, but the person who humbles himself will later be honored (Matthew 23:12).

These are not easy things to do. It isn't natural for us to consider the needs of others before our own. The only way we are able to do so is by following the model of Christ. Jesus was able to serve others without regard for receiving service in return because he was so completely secure in his identity. We see this clearly in John 13 in which Jesus performed the visual parable of washing the feet of the disciples.

The Scriptures tell us that Jesus understood three things before he assumed the role of a lowly servant and began to wash his disciples' feet: He understood where he had come from, that

all things had been given to him, and where his final destiny
would lead him (John 13:3). In other words, he understood his
true identity, his true dignity, and his true significance. He knew
who he was, why he had come, and where he was going.
That's why Paul wrote to the believers in Philippi,

> Your attitude should be the same as that of Christ
> Jesus:
>   Who, being in very nature God, did not consider
> equality with God something to be grasped, but made
> himself nothing, taking the very nature of a servant,
> being made in human likeness.
>   And being found in appearance as a man, he
> humbled himself and became obedient to death—
> even death on a cross! (Philippians 2:5–8)

So far, this not a very inspirational text. But this is just the
first part. Exaltation follows humility:

> Therefore God exalted him to the highest place and
> gave him the name that is above every name, that at
> the name of Jesus every knee should bow, in heaven
> and on earth and under the earth, and every tongue
> confess that Jesus Christ is Lord, to the glory of God
> the Father. (Philippians 2:9–11)

From this beautiful passage we learn three things about our
Lord that model for us the essence of true humility. First, Jesus
didn't selfishly cling to the outer expression of his divinity.
Instead, he took the form of a servant. Second, Jesus demonstrated his humility through obedience to the Father. Instead of
trying to impose his will on God, he submitted to God's will for
him. Third, Jesus waited for his Father to lift him up. He didn't
grab for power; he patiently waited for God to provide the
increase in his time. And now, seated in power at the right hand
of God, he intercedes on our behalf (Acts 5:29–32). As the perfect model for godly leadership, Jesus set the perfect example of

humility. Honor comes from God, and it comes—as counter-intuitive as it seems—as the result of downward mobility. Jesus chose downward mobility, a descent from the heights of heaven to a teenager's womb to a cattle trough to a peasant home to a dusty road to a cross to a tomb. Jesus didn't surrender a little; he surrendered everything, completely confident that his Father would take care of the outcome. The most powerful person who ever walked on the planet calls us and says: "I served you, and now I am asking you to serve others. A servant is not greater than his master. If I did this for you, you must do this for one another. I will take care of your dignity. You don't have to take yourself so seriously, because I take you seriously."

Anyone can claim to be a servant, but Jesus Christ, the Son of the living God, was treated as one and never complained about it. Jesus Christ, the most powerful man ever to walk on the face of the earth, was also the most humble man who ever lived. His agenda was never to promote himself, but to please his Father by loving and serving others. We are called to emulate that humility.

HUMILITY AND HONOR

Richard Foster, in his book *Celebration of Discipline*, writes, "More than any other single way, the grace of humility is worked in our lives through the discipline of serving."[3] Foster recalled how his friend, the late Jamie Buckingham, took this sentiment even further, insisting that you'll really know you are a true servant when you have a positive reaction toward people when they treat you like one.

In other words, the true test of humility comes when we are treated like a servant. It is one thing to choose to serve others, but it is another thing entirely to choose to be a servant. A servant is often taken for granted, overlooked, unnoticed. A servant gives up the right to be in charge of whom he serves, when he serves, and how long he serves. Everything in us screams out against such service, especially if it is rendered in secret. Our society has trained us well in the art of assertiveness, and we fear anything that even remotely resembles passivity or servility. The notion of being taken advantage of is abhorrent to us, and we most fear becoming something akin to the old comic strip character Casper Milquetoast, a walking doormat with no assurance or strength.

On the contrary, humility, biblically speaking, actually comes from disciplined strength and others-centered power. It is, in fact, the strength and understanding of our great dignity and identity in Christ. It is only through our willingness to serve that we can avoid manipulating people to get our needs met. Because of our new identity in Christ, we can serve without needing to be noticed or rewarded here on earth. We can do so because we understand that we serve One who always sees and who has promised to reward us in eternity (Ephesians 6:8).

When we trust God enough to take him at his word, it is evidence that we know that God's plans for us are "plans to prosper [us] and not to harm [us], plans to give [us] hope and a future" (Jeremiah 29:11).

God longs to bless and reward his people, but it is essential that as his people we be willing to turn to him and repent of our unfaithfulness and disobedience, as he tells us in his Word, "You will seek me and find me when you seek me with *all* your heart" (Jeremiah 29:13). We serve a God who "rewards those who earnestly seek him" (Hebrews 11:6). God actually enjoys bestowing benefits on those who turn to him in dependence and trust (cf. Psalm 35:27; Luke 12:32).

Humility in the Face of Success

Perks and privileges usually accompany successful leadership. Many leaders enjoy being in charge, making decisions that affect the organization, delegating implementation of those decisions to others, "running the show," having others defer to them in meetings and the like. As one gets ahead, it's hard not to get a big head!

As a leader, King Solomon enjoyed all these perks and much more. Like few leaders before or since, he had wealth, power, fame, wisdom, and plenty of servants. Other rulers traveled long distances to listen to his wisdom, and other entrepreneurs came to marvel at his wealth. Yet from this lofty position Solomon cautioned, "It is not good ... nor is it honorable to seek one's own honor" (Proverbs 25:27). Doing so, he warned, is like eating too much honey. Sweet as it is, and healthy as it is in proper amounts, too much of this good thing will make us sick—and sick of it.

Honor accompanies a job well done. If a leader is effective, he will get all the honor he can stand. But a person who has to go looking for honor has his hand in the wrong hive. Solomon learned that focusing on a job well done is the way to earn honor. Focusing on honor cuts into the time and energy needed to do the job well.

Most of our lives, we have a hidden impact. Most of our lives, we don't know our impact. Every so often, God will show us our impact—through a word of encouragement or a note of appreciation when we are down. Every so often, we may get a little positive feedback, just enough to let us know that we are on the right course. But if God gives us too much of that kind of acknowledgment, we start to live for it—which is a dangerous path to walk. In John 5:44 Jesus asked a pointed question with which we would do well to wrestle: "How can you believe if you accept praise from one another, yet make no effort to obtain the praise that comes from the only God?"

If we seek praise from others rather than from God, we will live in constant insecurity. We all know what insecure people are like. Always searching for approval, they are never able to relax. They are driven by an unending quest for perfection that torments them and everyone around them. Often, their self-esteem is tied to their material possessions; to them it is so important to always have something a little bit newer, a little bit better, a little bit bigger than what others have. Because insecurity and envy often go together, they relentlessly find fault with others. Their pride compels them to continually seek a higher place; their envy makes them constantly resentful of others' good fortune. Insecure people are so focused on image rather than substance that they have a distinct and identifiable *persona* about them. In their minds and hearts they have an image that they feel they must sustain, and our culture supports that feeling. As surprising as it may seem, insecure people are often proud, and proud people are defensive. They cannot handle criticism or rebuke. They cannot receive instruction or correction; therefore, it is hard for them to be teachable, because they always have to defend their self-image, their pride of person, place, and position.

Humility in the Face of Prosperity

One of the great dangers of material success is that we deceive ourselves into the arrogant belief that we ourselves have brought it about. We are like Bart Simpson who prays at the dinner table, "Dear God, we paid for all this stuff ourselves, so thanks for nothing."

God can give prosperity, and he can give poverty. He can raise us up; he can bring us down (Psalm 75:6–7). Sometimes it is the severe mercy of God to impoverish us because we are getting too cocky. He may need to take away some of our toys until we get the message.

We are all born with closed hands. Babies come into the world with their hands balled up into tiny little fists. As we grow older, we learn to hold tightly to things—other people's hands, handlebars and lunchboxes, bats and balls, girlfriends and boyfriends, gadgets and gizmos, trophies and medals, ratings and rankings, money and membership. When we start out in the business world, we grab the lowest rung on the corporate ladder, and we hold on for dear life until we can clutch the next one. We clutch and scrape for whatever position or prestige we can garner. Perhaps one day we will find ourselves hanging on to canes and walkers or even the edge of a hospital bed. We cling tightly to life itself until we die. Then, perhaps because our focus will no longer be on ourselves and this earthly realm, we can finally relax our grip. What a contrast between our hands and the hands of God. Throughout the Bible story God opens his hands to provide food, protection, blessing, love, and support. The psalmist wrote of God, "You open your hand and satisfy the desires of every living thing" (Psalm 145:16). When God came to this earth in the person of Jesus of Nazareth, he taught, loved, and blessed. But mostly he opened his hands and touched. He refused to clutch or cling tightly to his rights and privileges. Instead, he opened his hands and, in the most startling example of humility the world has ever known, stretched out his arms on the cross to pay for our failures.

THE HUMILITY OF MOSES

If Jesus was the perfect example of humility in the New Testament, Moses personified humility in the Old Testament. In Numbers 12:3 there is a parenthetical statement that was inserted into the text: "(Now Moses was a very humble man, more humble than anyone else on the face of the earth.)" Moses was a man of authority and power and charisma, but he manifested this disciplined strength through his utter willingness to be pleasing to the Father.

In Isaiah 57:15 God says, "I live in a high and holy place, but also with him who is contrite and lowly in spirit, to revive the spirit of the lowly and to revive the heart of the contrite." Later in Isaiah 66:2, he states, "This is the one I esteem: he who is humble and contrite in spirit, and trembles at my word." The Bible repeatedly emphasizes that "God opposes the proud but gives grace to the humble" (see James 4:6; 1 Peter 5:5; cf. Psalm 138:6; Proverbs 3:34; Matthew 23:12). Those who are proud have an inappropriate and inflated view of themselves. They attribute their accomplishments to their own efforts and fail to acknowledge that everything they are and have comes directly from God's hand.

One way to summarize the Bible's message is that in it God is telling us, "I am God, and you are not." The quality of humility flows out of a proper assessment of ourselves before God. Moses was a powerful man, but he was also a humble man because he saw himself in the light of God and sought God's honor and reputation, not his own.

Moses had obviously come to grips with his desperate need for the grace and mercy of God, as evidenced by four characteristics: First, he had a teachable spirit. Humble people understand that they are constantly under construction.

Second, he was willing to seek wise counsel. Humble people are never too proud to seek out the wisdom of others before making important decisions. The Bible advises, "Plans fail for lack of counsel, but with many advisers they succeed" (Proverbs 15:22).

Third, he was willing to submit to authority. Ultimately, we all must submit to the authority of God, but we must also yield to the authority of those he has placed over us—pastors, elders, government leaders.

Fourth, he didn't have a sense of entitlement. Israel's pride led them to disobey God's commands, so God invested forty years in developing their humility and obedience, as evidenced in Moses' words to them on the eve of their entry into the Promised Land:

> When you have eaten and are satisfied, praise the
> LORD your God for the good land he has given you.
> Be careful that you do not forget the LORD your God,
> failing to observe his commands, his laws and his
> decrees that I am giving you this day. Otherwise,
> when you eat and are satisfied, when you build fine
> houses and settle down, and when your herds and
> flocks grow large and your silver and gold increase
> and all you have is multiplied, then your heart will
> become proud and you will forget the LORD your

God, who brought you out of Egypt, out of the land of slavery.... You may say to yourself, "My power and the strength of my hands have produced this wealth for me." But remember the LORD your God, for it is he who gives you the ability to produce wealth, and so confirms his covenant, which he swore to your forefathers, as it is today.
(Deuteronomy 8:10–14, 17–18)

Moses exhorted the people to remember, after they have taken the land and flourished, that everything they have has come to them as a gift from the Lord. Humble people walk gratefully before their God and do not think they have achieved anything in and of themselves (cf. Micah 6:8).

HUMILITY PRECEDES ELEVATION

Late in his life, Peter, as an older, wiser leader in the church, wrote, "Humble yourselves, therefore, under God's mighty hand, that he may lift you up in due time. Cast all your anxiety on him because he cares for you" (1 Peter 5:6–7). Anxiety builds up in all forms from time to time. When it does, it is a sign that we have taken a burden back on ourselves that we were never meant to carry. We can give it back to God and put ourselves under his mighty hand, knowing that he cares for us and that he will provide the recognition we deserve at the proper time. Nothing that we do for his pleasure will go unrecognized.

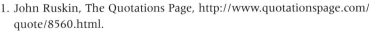

1. John Ruskin, The Quotations Page, http://www.quotationspage.com/quote/8560.html.
2. Thomas Alexander Fyfe, *Who's Who in Dickens* (Ann Arbor, MI: Gryphon, 1971), 267.
3. Richard Foster, *Celebration of Discipline* (San Francisco: HarperSanFrancisco, 1971), 130.

CHAPTER 6

Commitment

FULLY COMMITTED

A chicken and a pig were walking down the road together. They passed a sign for a local diner advertising its breakfast special: "Ham and Eggs—$3.95!" The chicken said, "That's our whole contribution to society: breakfast food!" The pig replied, "For you, it may be a contribution. For me it's a total commitment."

Life in the modern world has programmed us to expect a life of ease. It is not merely that we want everything to be easy; who wouldn't want that? What is troubling is that we now expect to receive abundant rewards with minimal effort. If something requires effort or time, it must not be meant to be, and we feel thoroughly justified in avoiding it or giving it up. Worse yet are those who believe legitimate goals may be sought through illegitimate means, provided that those means offer a shortcut to the goal in mind.

Take, for example, the professional athlete who chooses to illegally enhance his performance through the use of steroids. Not only does he cheapen himself, he also robs his fellow athletes of any kind of fair competition. He does so simply because he does not want to put in the time and effort necessary to better himself honestly.

This kind of selfishness is a dangerous character trait to develop. Common sense reveals that some of the best things in life demand effort and prove worthy of whatever amount of time or labor is endured in their pursuit. The best relationships require work. The best businesses are built on the blood, sweat, and tears of their leaders. Even spiritual growth is reflective of faithful investment. G. K. Chesterton once quipped, "The Christian ideal has not been tried and found wanting. It has been found difficult, and left untried."[1]

Of course, this situation is nothing new. Thousands of years ago, God asked, "Who is he who will devote himself to be close to me?" (Jeremiah 30:21). We don't want to hear it, but the fact of the matter is that following God involves sacrifice, effort, devotion. We much prefer the spiritual growth plans that guarantee complete maturity in "15 minutes a day!"

Mark Oppenheimer has written of the proliferation of these mistaken ideas regarding what is truly involved in personal life change. These deficient notions can be found in everything from the *Chicken Soup for the Soul* books to WWJD bracelets to the awe-inspiring angelic visitations received in the lives of television characters. It all sounds good, but there is never any kind of demand or call for commitment or life change involved. "Just Do It" doesn't really mean, "Just run one hundred miles every week like marathon runners do." "Just Do It" means, "Just buy the shoes—swift feet sure to follow."[2] As if anyone will become magically fit simply by purchasing the proper athletic footwear.

Leaders know that it is not so. Leaders know that such behavior used to have a name; it was called "sloth." In "The Other Six Deadly Sins," Dorothy Sayers wrote,

> In the world it is called tolerance, but in hell it is
> called despair. It is the accomplice of the other sins
> and their worst punishment. It is the sin which
> believes in nothing, cares for nothing, seeks to know
> nothing, finds purpose in nothing, lives for nothing,
> and only remains alive because there is nothing it

would die for. We have known it far too well for
many years. The only thing perhaps that we have not
known about it is that it is mortal sin.[3]

Leaders know the truth of Theodore Roosevelt's words: "Far
better it is to dare mighty things, to win glorious triumphs even
though checkered by failure, than to rank with those poor spirits
who neither enjoy nor suffer much because they live in the gray
twilight that knows neither victory nor defeat."[4] There is a great
danger in our time of succumbing to mediocrity not through
incompetence or a lack of integrity but simply from a lack of genuine commitment. To live without such commitment is to live in
that "gray twilight that knows neither victory nor defeat."

Godly men and women understand that effective leadership
flows from being deeply committed to the right things. As followers of Christ, the single most important commitment of our
lives is, obviously, to God. Any lasting success we experience as
leaders will flow from that commitment, which is why the apostle Paul wrote:

> Therefore, I urge you, brothers, in view of God's
> mercy, to offer your bodies as living sacrifices, holy
> and pleasing to God—this is your spiritual act of wor-
> ship. Do not conform any longer to the pattern of
> this world, but be transformed by the renewing of
> your mind. Then you will be able to test and approve
> what God's will is—his good, pleasing and perfect
> will. (Romans 12:1–2)

The word "Therefore" in this passage points to all the apostle has written in the preceding eleven chapters. In light of God's
mercy, which justifies, sanctifies, and will someday glorify us,
we are to offer ourselves as living sacrifices to him. In other
words, we should allow God's mercy to accomplish this addi-
tional work in our lives. We should let it drive us to absolute
commitment.

Those who have been taken captive by the love of God will affirm the lordship of Jesus Christ in their lives by heeding this call to "offer your bodies as living sacrifices, holy and pleasing to God" (12:1). The word "offer" implies that this act, much like a wedding vow, occurs once. It may be renewed, but at some point we should be motivated by God's mercy to devote ourselves to him. When we take this step, we are acknowledging Christ's leadership in our lives. We sacrifice our selfish desires and misguided ambitions as we strive to align ourselves with God's will. Once this act of commitment occurs, our talents and dreams will be surrendered to his purpose. And the more we give ourselves to him, the more he will bless us and use us.

The sequence here is vitally important. In the Old Testament, there were two broad categories of sacrifice that might be offered to God under different circumstances. There were atonement sacrifices and celebration sacrifices. Atonement sacrifices were for the covering of sin with blood and the reconciliation of people with God or one another. These sacrifices were offered as a response to sin and guilt.

On the other hand, the Law of Moses also made provision for sacrifices of joy. When the crops were harvested, when a child was born, when a great deliverance occurred—the people would come before God to offer gifts of thanksgiving and celebration.

Christians acknowledge one and only one atonement sacrifice: Jesus himself. But we engage in perpetual sacrifices of celebration and thanksgiving to the God who has saved us. While it is true that we offer God our time, talents, abilities, and money, the most fundamental sacrifice we give him is our very bodies. Paul, the writer of this text, would not abide abstract or ethereal religion. Our bodies are the instruments of all our actions in this world. Therefore, it is our bodies that must be yielded to God in every area.

We naturally expect people to conform to their environment. The phrase most often used in this vein is, "When in Rome, do as the Romans do." Those of us who have been justified, sanctified,

and consecrated to God, however, face a different set of expecta-
tions. We who have received God's grace and been transported
out of darkness into his kingdom of marvelous light (Colossians
1:13) will be shaped and molded by our new experience. Such an
overwhelming experience is bound to have an impact on our
lives. That is only logical.

In fact, the word translated "spiritual" is the Greek term
logikos. The word fundamentally means "rational" or "reasonable." In view of the mercy of God toward us, it is only rational or
reasonable that we should give our hearts, minds, and bodies to
be shaped by his gracious control. In view of the personal relationship God has purchased and established with us, no mere
ceremony or ritual is enough to offer him; he deserves the intelligent and rational surrender of every fiber of our being to him.

THE GOD WHO COMMITS

Douglas Rumford makes a profound statement in his book
Soul Shaping. He writes, "We make our commitments, then
our commitments make us. Once they are chosen, many other
choices follow as a matter of course."[5] Once we commit to follow Jesus, many other decisions in life must fall into line or we
will overturn our prior commitment.

But how are we to know that our commitment to God will be
honored? All of the commitments we make should flow from the
commitment God has first made to us. Once God committed himself to our highest good, his will toward us was sealed. God tells
us that he is committed to all who are in Christ, and that our relationship with him will last forever. Jeremiah 31:31–36 reveals the
covenant of commitment the Lord made with his people:

> "The time is coming," declares the LORD, "when I will
> make a new covenant with the house of Israel and
> with the house of Judah. It will not be like the
> covenant I made with their forefathers when I took

them by the hand to lead them out of Egypt, because they broke my covenant, though I was a husband to them," declares the LORD.

"This is the covenant I will make with the house of Israel after that time," declares the LORD. "I will put my law in their minds and write it on their hearts. I will be their God, and they will be my people. No longer will a man teach his neighbor, or a man his brother, saying, 'Know the LORD,' because they will all know me, from the least of them to the greatest," declares the LORD. "For I will forgive their wickedness and will remember their sins no more."

This is what the LORD says, he who appoints the sun to shine by day, who decrees the moon and stars to shine by night, who stirs up the sea so that its waves roar—the LORD Almighty is his name: "Only if these decrees vanish from my sight," declares the LORD, "will the descendants of Israel ever cease to be a nation before me."

The ultimate basis for security and significance in life relates to commitment (security) and to the length of time something will last (significance). In these six verses, God provided for his people a sense of both security and significance—a sure word that his commitment to them would never fail.

In spite of the rebelliousness of the people of Judah, the Lord assured them through the prophet Jeremiah that he was committed to their ultimate good. Judgment was inevitable because they had flagrantly violated God's commands, but the prophet looked beyond this impending condemnation to a time of consolation. There would be a faithful remnant, and God's people would eventually enjoy the blessings of forgiveness and complete renewal.

In this covenant, God committed himself to the welfare of the house of Israel and Judah and predicted a time when they would all know him and when his law would be written on their hearts. "'For I know the plans I have for you,' declares the Lord, 'plans to prosper you and not to harm you, plans to give you hope and a future'" (Jeremiah 29:11).

God's grace always precedes our response and demonstrates his unshakable commitment to us. "This is how God showed his love among us: He sent his one and only Son into the world that we might live through him. This is love: not that we loved God, but that he loved us and sent his Son as an atoning sacrifice for our sins" (1 John 4:9–10). When we love God, it is "because he first loved us" (1 John 4:19).

Lewis Thomas, scientist and philosopher, described humans best when he said: "We are, perhaps, uniquely among earth's creatures, the worrying animal. We worry away our lives, fearing the future, discontent with the present, unable to take in the idea of dying, unable to sit still."[6] God's promise of abiding love and commitment to our well-being enables us to live above worry, above fear. His commitment to us empowers us to follow through on our commitment to him. As Martin Luther said, "It is not imitation which brings about our sonship of God, but our sonship which makes possible imitation."[7]

The Rewards of Commitment

As leaders, how are we to demonstrate and practice commitment? Jesus reveals his standard of deeper commitment in Matthew's gospel:

> Then Jesus said to his disciples, "If anyone would come after me, he must deny himself and take up his cross and follow me. For whoever wants to save his life will lose it, but whoever loses his life for me will find it. What good will it be for a man if he gains the whole world, yet forfeits his soul? Or what can a man give in exchange for his soul?" (Matthew 16:24–26)

Jesus spoke these words to his disciples, but they still call us to action today. Through these living words, Jesus made it clear that he requires total commitment of his followers. He said that unless one commits everything, one loses everything. As Christian leaders, that commitment must remain strong until the end of our earthly walk. Inspirational and motivational speaker Og Mandino expands on the necessity of strong, long-term commitment. One of Mandino's ten common causes of failure is "quitting too soon." Mandino tells the story of Raphael Solano and his companions, who were looking for diamonds in a dry riverbed in Venezuela. Discouraged, and facing the thought of returning home to his very poor family empty-handed, Solano claimed he had picked up about 999,999 rocks and was quitting. His companions said, "Pick up one more and make it a million." That "millionth" rock was the 155-carat "Liberator." Mandino writes,

> I think he [Solano] must have known a happiness
> that went beyond the financial. He had set his
> course; the odds were against him; he had perse-
> vered; he had won. He had not only done what he
> had set out to do—which is a reward in itself—but he
> had done it in the face of failure and obscurity.[8]

Jesus urged his followers, "Take up your cross and follow me." He knew better than anyone else how elusive the great prize is. But he also knew that anything less than a total commitment to achieving the prize would not suffice. In the Christian life, as in the leader's organizational life, total commitment to the cause facilitates success.

COMMITTED TO GOD

High-quality relationships are founded on the solid rock of commitment, not the shifting sand of feelings or emotions. God calls us to be people of commitment, first to him and then to others. As a great leader of Israel, Joshua's entire life was marked by commitment. We even hear this commitment in his final words to the people under his leadership:

> "Now fear the LORD and serve him with all faithfulness. Throw away the gods your forefathers worshiped beyond the River and in Egypt, and serve the LORD. But if serving the LORD seems undesirable to you, then choose for yourselves this day whom you will serve, whether the gods your forefathers served beyond the River, or the gods of the Amorites, in whose land you are living. But as for me and my household, we will serve the LORD."
>
> Then the people answered, "Far be it from us to forsake the LORD to serve other gods! It was the LORD our God himself who brought us and our fathers up out of Egypt, from that land of slavery, and performed those great signs before our eyes. He protected us on our entire journey and among all the nations through which we traveled. And the LORD drove out before us all the nations, including the Amorites, who lived in the land. We too will serve the LORD, because he is our God."
>
> Joshua said to the people, "You are not able to serve the LORD. He is a holy God; he is a jealous God. He will not forgive your rebellion and your sins. If you forsake the LORD and serve foreign gods, he will turn and bring disaster on you and make an end of you, after he has been good to you."
>
> But the people said to Joshua, "No! We will serve the LORD."
>
> Then Joshua said, "You are witnesses against yourselves that you have chosen to serve the LORD."
>
> "Yes, we are witnesses," they replied.
>
> "Now then," said Joshua, "throw away the foreign gods that are among you and yield your hearts

to the LORD, the God of Israel."
And the people said to Joshua, "We will serve
the LORD our God and obey him."
On that day Joshua made a covenant for the
people, and there at Shechem he drew up for them
decrees and laws. And Joshua recorded these things
in the Book of the Law of God. Then he took a large
stone and set it up there under the oak near the holy
place of the LORD.
"See!" he said to all the people. "This stone will
be a witness against us. It has heard all the words the
LORD has said to us. It will be a witness against you if
you are untrue to your God." (Joshua 24:14–27)

Joshua told the people that even if they chose not to serve
the Lord, they would still not be exempt from service.

SINGLE-MINDEDNESS

If we do not serve the Creator, we will unavoidably serve some
part of the creation. But the gods of success, position, and
possessions are cruel taskmasters and never deliver the profound satisfaction they promise. God alone is the worthy object
of our total commitment, and if we direct our highest commitment to anything else, we commit idolatry. We were designed to
serve God and to find our deepest satisfaction in him, but we
will be halfhearted at best if we try to play by two sets of rules
and serve two masters (Luke 16:13).

In the 1991 movie *City Slickers*, Billy Crystal plays Mitch—a
confused, dissatisfied man with a vague sense that life is passing
him by. Jack Palance plays the ancient sage Curly—"a saddlebag
with eyes." At a critical moment in the film, Curly asks Mitch if
he would like to know the secret of life.

"It's this," Curly says, holding up his index finger.

"The secret of life is your finger?" asks Mitch.

"It's *one thing*," Curly replies. "The secret of life is one thing—just one thing."

Something about this statement strikes a chord deep within Mitch. His life is a mess; he feels pulled by his obligations to his family and his desire for fulfillment at his work—torn between his need for security and his longing for excitement. Like many men, Mitch is divided. His life is about too many different things. Thus, he feels it is about nothing.

He asks Curly to tell him what that one thing is, but the best Curly can do is to tell Mitch, "You have to find it for yourself."

Believe it or not, the wise old cowboy is parroting Danish philosopher Søren Kierkegaard, who saw double-mindedness as the primary affliction of modern man. His book *Purity of Heart Is to Will One Thing* is a meditation on the biblical statement: "Purify your hearts, you double-minded" (James 4:8). The sickness, according to Kierkegaard, is really a failure to achieve an integrated life, a life that is focused on one thing. It is the failure to make an ultimate commitment to "the Good," to "seeking first the kingdom of God."[9]

Many of those who followed Jesus were merely curious. Others were convinced of the truth of what he was teaching, but only a few were fully and personally committed to him. When his uncommitted followers began to leave him in response to his difficult sayings, Jesus turned to the twelve disciples and asked if they wanted to leave with the others. Although it is doubtful that they understood the Lord any better than those who were leaving, they realized that once having committed themselves to him, there was no turning back (John 6:60–69). As disciples of Christ, we are called to remain committed to him, even when we don't fully understand all of his plans for us. Failure to do so leads to misery and a lack of effectiveness in ministry. As François Fénelon wrote,

> Woe to those weak and timid souls who are divided
> between God and their world! They want and they
> do not want. They are torn by desire and remorse at

the same time.... They have a horror of evil and a shame of good. They have the pains of virtue without tasting its sweet consolations. O how wretched they are.[10]

As godly leaders, "[We] are witnesses against [ourselves] that [we] have chosen to serve the LORD" (Joshua 24:22). Have we assessed how that commitment has been played out in our lives? In what ways has our level of commitment to the Lord been conditioned by our understanding of what he is doing in our lives? The call to commitment is a call to constant vigilance in maintaining and understanding the standards of that commitment. No matter what distractions we may encounter, we need to maintain our focus on serving the Lord.

Committing Versus Bargaining

How on earth do leaders establish and retain committed followers? How, in some cases, do we get ourselves committed enough to pay the high price of success? God knows how, and the prophet Habakkuk modeled an essential truth about God-focused commitment:

> Though the fig tree does not bud and there are no
> grapes on the vines, though the olive crop fails and
> the fields produce no food, though there are no
> sheep in the pen and no cattle in the stalls, yet I will
> rejoice in the LORD, I will be joyful in God my Savior.
> (Habakkuk 3:17–18)

What a refreshing statement! Many leaders would love to have followers who are this committed to the cause. In fact, many leaders would love to have this level of commitment to their *own* cause. The key ingredient to Habakkuk's statement is that it is unidirectional; he promised to maintain his attitude regardless of the payback.

That's really what "commitment" is. The statement, "I will

be committed if" isn't commitment making; it's deal making. It's not committing; it's bargaining. In Habakkuk 2:2–20, God explained his justice and his majesty to the prophet. The passage above is the prophet's response to that revelation of God's character.

In the absence of a life-consuming ideal, asking for the level of commitment Habakkuk expressed is absurd. As leaders we must identify what it is within our organizations that is genuinely worthy of commitment. Until we complete this definition, we will sound rather shallow even talking about it. No sane person will commit to things that don't really matter. But when an organization's goals and outcomes are properly related to the living God and its activities honor him, then commitment makes sense. Instead of asking, "How do we get commitment?" we should begin by asking, "To what (or whom) are we committed?"

1. G. K. Chesterton, *The Collected Works of G. K. Chesterton*, ed. George Marlin (San Francisco: Ignatius, 1987), 4:61.
2. Mark Oppenheimer, "Salvation Without Sacrifice," *Charlotte Observer*, 30 October 2000, sec. 11A.
3. Dorothy Sayers, *The Other Six Deadly Sins: An Address Given to the Public Morality Council at Claxton Hall, Westminster, on October 23rd, 1941* (London: Methuen, 1943).
4. Theodore Roosevelt, "Speech before the Hamilton Club," in *The Strenuous Life*, 5th ed. (Bedford, MA: Applewood Books, 1991).
5. Douglas J. Rumford, *Soul Shaping* (Wheaton, IL: Tyndale, 1996), 91.
6. *The Medusa and the Snail*, quoted in *Bartlett's Familiar Quotations,* 15th ed., ed. Emily Morison Beck (Boston: Little, Brown, 1980), 884.
7. Quoted in Gordon S. Wakefield, *The Westminster Dictionary of Christian Spirituality* (Philadelphia: Westminster Press, 1983), 209.
8. Adapted from Og Mandino's *University of Success* (New York: Bantam Books, 1982), 44–45.
9. Søren Kierkegaard, *Purity of Heart Is to Will One Thing* (New York: Harper Bros., 1938).
10. François Fénelon, *Christian Perfection*, quoted in Richard Foster and J. B. Smith, eds., *Devotional Classics* (San Francisco: HarperCollins, 1993), 48.

Part 2:

THE SKILLS SEEN IN
THE PERFECT LEADER

CHAPTER 7

Vision Casting

THE IMPORTANCE OF COMMUNICATION

A man was struggling to get his washing machine through the front door of his home as his neighbor was walking past. The neighbor, being a *good* neighbor, stopped and asked if he could help. The man breathed a sigh of relief and said, "That would be great. I'll get it from the inside, and you get it from the outside. We should be able to handle this quickly."

But after five minutes of continual struggle, they were both exhausted. Wiping the sweat from his brow, the neighbor said, "This thing is bigger than it looks. I don't know if we'll ever be able to get it into your house."

"*Into* my house?" said the man. "I'm trying to get this thing *out* of my house!"

Few things are more vital than clear communication, particularly for leaders. The great Italian conductor Arturo Toscanini was notoriously bad at communicating what he wanted to his musicians. His fits of frustration at his own lack of communication skills were legendary. After trying several times to convey something very particular to a trumpet player, he threw up his hands and shouted, "God tells me how the music should sound, but you stand in the way!" On another occasion, during a rehearsal of Debussy's *La Mer*, he found himself yet again at a loss for words to describe the effect he hoped to achieve from a particular passage. He thought for a moment, then took a silk handkerchief from his pocket and tossed it high in the air. The mesmerized musicians watched its slow and graceful descent through the air. "There," said the maestro, "play it like that."[1]

It is one thing to have vision, but without clear communication, vision will never become reality. Until others have understood the vision well enough to articulate it themselves, they cannot be expected to pursue it with passion. Leonard Sweet wisely reminds us, "It's not people who are right who change the world. It's people who can communicate their definition of right to others who change the world."[2]

MAKING SURE THE VISION IS "CAUGHT"

Obviously, when communication breaks down, there can be a number of problems. The problem may be in transmission. As we have just seen, trying to transfer something before it is truly in our possession leads to a breakdown in communication. But sometimes the problem is in the reception. For example, God had a great vision that he wanted Moses to "catch." But he encountered resistance when he communicated his vision to his reluctant servant. Through this story we learn a great deal about how to help those who don't "buy into" a vision when they first hear it. Despite Moses' initial strong resistance, God finally "sold him" on the vision.

Every leader occasionally faces seemingly impossible challenges. The opposition appears too strong, too entrenched, and too well organized. The leader's own resources seem too small by comparison. That's how Moses must have felt when God appeared to him in the burning bush:

> The LORD said, "I have indeed seen the misery of my
> people in Egypt. I have heard them crying out

because of their slave drivers, and I am concerned about their suffering. So I have come down to rescue them from the hand of the Egyptians and to bring them up out of that land into a good and spacious land, a land flowing with milk and honey.... And now the cry of the Israelites has reached me, and I have seen the way the Egyptians are oppressing them. So now, go. I am sending you to Pharaoh to bring my people the Israelites out of Egypt." (Exodus 3:7–10)

Moses responded to God's call with three questions and two objections that expressed his unbelief and lack of confidence. First, Moses asked, "Who am I?" (v. 11). That question revealed a radical change in Moses. Forty years earlier, Moses had impulsively taken it upon himself to vindicate a fellow Hebrew for a beating the Hebrew had endured from an Egyptian (2:11–12). Now Moses felt inadequate for the task before him, even though God himself was commissioning him. God's response was exactly what Moses needed: "And God said, 'I will be with you. And this will be the sign to you that it is I who have sent you: When you have brought the people out of Egypt, you will worship God on this mountain'" (3:12). Moses would soon discover that one plus God equals a majority.

Moses' second question was about the identity of the One who was sending him to undertake this daunting task: "What shall I tell them?" (v. 13). Convincing more than two million slaves that he had been sent to lead them out of bondage was a tall order. Moses would need an authority higher than himself to persuade them to follow him. In response to this second question, again God gave Moses what he needed: "God said to Moses, 'I am who I am. This is what you are to say to the Israelites: "I AM has sent me to you"'" (v. 14). By calling himself "I AM," God revealed his identity as the eternal God who is always there for his people. He told Moses to tell the Israelites that he was the God of Abraham and the God of Isaac (v. 15), a description that he knew would resonate with the Hebrew slaves in Egypt.

Still unconvinced, Moses asked a third question: "What if they do not believe me?" (4:1). Moses no doubt remembered what had happened forty years earlier. While Moses was trying to settle a dispute between two Hebrew men, one of them had scornfully asked, "Who made you ruler and judge over us?" (2:14). With those words still echoing in his mind, it is understandable that Moses would fear rejection. But God told Moses that he would validate his leadership through a series of miracles that would convince even the most skeptical person in Egypt. As long as Moses stayed at God's side, he would have no cause for worry.

With Moses' first and second objections, he implied that he wasn't qualified to lead the people to freedom because he wasn't an eloquent speaker (4:10) and that therefore God should choose someone else (4:13). At this point Moses' fear of failure prevailed over his memory. So many years had passed since Moses had used any leadership skills that he thought he had lost them. Once more God responded to Moses with compassion. God promised to give him words to say and then deputized Aaron to help him:

> The LORD said to him, "Who gave man his mouth?
> Who makes him deaf or mute? Who gives him sight
> or makes him blind? Is it not I, the LORD? Now go; I
> will help you speak and will teach you what to
> say.... What about your brother, Aaron the Levite? I
> know he can speak well. He is already on his way
> to meet you, and his heart will be glad when he
> sees you. You shall speak to him and put words in
> his mouth; I will help both of you speak and will
> teach you what to do. He will speak to the people
> for you, and it will be as if he were your mouth and
> as if you were God to him." (Exodus 4:11–12,
> 14–16)

Moses was about to become one of the greatest leaders of world history. When God directed him to lead in a difficult situation, Moses hesitated before he obeyed—but he did obey. God showed Moses genuine understanding of his fears and concerns about what God wanted him to contribute to this overwhelming vision. God addressed each of Moses' questions and statements and assured him of strength and success. As Moses' concerns went away, so did his resistance to the vision. Like Moses, even the best of the people we are called to lead will hesitate when they face seemingly impossible situations. At such times they need to know that their leader understands their fears and still believes they will succeed in the task before them.

How exactly did God lead Moses from resisting the vision of deliverance to leading it? Let's review the five points of resistance to the vision and God's response to each point.

"Who am I?" (3:11). This sense of being overwhelmed should accompany any well-formed vision statement. If the statement doesn't have a sense of the ridiculous about it, and if the hearers don't, at least initially, feel they are in over their heads, then there is no challenge, no spark to call them to stretch and push. But the strength of the vision statement will both stimulate and overcome resistance. To Moses' question, "Who am I?" God said in effect, "You are the person I have called to fulfill this mission. But what is important is not who *you* are, but who *I* am and what *I* want you to do" (3:1–12).

"What shall I tell them?" (3:13). This question reflects the concerns of cost and value. Moses was asking God, "Who's behind this? Who will accept the final responsibility for such an overwhelming vision?" Moses was looking for some authoritative backup. So will the people we are called to lead. When Moses asked God, "What shall I tell them?" God's response was, "Tell them that I am with you in this because you are fulfilling what I want done" (3:14–22).

"What if they don't believe me?" (4:1). Most people's reactions to vision statements go from a sense of being overwhelmed (point 1), to legitimate skepticism (point 2), to serious investigation of legitimacy. If a vision is stated well, people will demand evidence. "What if they don't believe me?" asked Moses. God answered: "Doubts are to be expected when presenting a grand vision. Give them enough evidence and rationale to help them address their doubts" (4:2–9).

"O Lord, I have never been eloquent" (4:10). This statement by Moses reflects the painful fact that people have tried great and glorious projects in the past, only to be disappointed or embarrassed. But people eagerly desire to invest their time and effort in successful ventures and will be motivated to do their best if consistently empowered to do so. "O Lord, I have not been eloquent," said Moses, to which God basically replied, "Trust me and let me show you what I can do through you" (4:11).

"Send someone else" (4:13). Moses' final resistance was, "Please, Lord, not me. I'm too overwhelmed. It's just easier to stay where I am." The leader who can effectively address this final appeal and get people excited about new possibilities will go a long way toward developing an effective team. "Please send someone else," Moses begged. But God persuaded Moses, urging his reluctant messenger to get on with the mission and trust his faithfulness. There is a time for persuasion and selling the vision, and a time for pushing to get it done.

ACTS 29

The most influential leader the world has ever known, Jesus of Nazareth, modeled vision casting for us. In fact, it could be said that the entire Bible is a vision-casting book that invites us not only to look ahead to God's promises for the future, but also to participate in their realization. God has granted us the immeasurable privilege of participating in his work, and he offers us "a slice of the action" that will have enduring consequences. James Emery White explained:

You were given life because God had a dream for
you. Individually, specifically, by name. You were no
accident. God willed you into existence, and He not
only gave you life, but He also invested you with
promise and potential. Within you is the opportunity
to join with God in fulfilling the great adventure
birthed in His mind for you from eternity.[3]

The book of Acts is the glorious story of Christ's vision being realized, but if we try to open our Bibles to Acts 29 we will discover that there is no Acts 29. The reason there is no Acts 29 in the Bible is because it is being written right now by each of us as the Good News of Jesus Christ is being proclaimed and lived out all over the world. In Acts 1:8, Luke (the author of Acts) gives us the outline for this volume through something Jesus told his followers just before his ascension: "You will receive power when the Holy Spirit comes on you; and you will be my witnesses in Jerusalem, and in all Judea and Samaria, and to the ends of the earth." We are active participants in that last phrase; we are witnesses charged with taking the life of Christ "to the ends of the earth."

At the end of Acts, Paul was under house arrest. He had made it to Rome, the center of culture and civilization in the first century. As such, Paul knew that if the gospel took root in Rome, it would spread all over the known world. So Luke recorded: "For two whole years Paul stayed there in his own rented house and welcomed all who came to see him. Boldly and without hindrance he preached the kingdom of God and taught about the Lord Jesus Christ" (Acts 28:30–31). That is how the narration ended.

Now, as modern-day readers of the book of Acts, when we get to this statement, we wonder what happened next. Did Paul make it to Caesar with his appeal? Did he live or was he executed? But Luke never told *the rest of the story....* What matters is that Paul had invested his entire life in helping God's glorious vision become a reality. And he handed the baton off to men like Timothy and Titus, and they in turn handed it off to faithful men and women who passed it to others. Down through the centuries the baton continued to be passed until someone placed it in our hands and said, "Go, be Christ's witness to the ends of the earth."

In the fourth chapter of his gospel, the apostle John records for us a time when Jesus imparted his vision to his disciples. After they returned from buying food, Jesus surprised them by telling them, "I have food to eat that you know nothing about" (John 4:32). At first they assumed he meant physical food, but he was referring to another kind of nourishment—that of participating in God's will: "My food ... is to do the will of him who sent me and to finish his work. Do you not say, 'Four months more and then the harvest'? I tell you, open your eyes and look at the fields! They are ripe for harvest" (vv. 34–35).

Before the disciples arrived on the scene, the Samaritan woman with whom Jesus had been talking had gone to tell the people of her village about the man who knew everything she had ever done. When Jesus told his disciples to look at the fields that were ripe for harvest, it may be that he was referring to the Samaritans who were on their way to talk with him. This passage illustrates how Jesus constantly sought to communicate to his followers a greater vision of the Father's will. Dr. Hans Finzel, executive director of a large church-planting organization, writes:

> Though much of my job as a CEO is communicating our vision and selling our dream out there among the public constituents, my insiders need to hear from me just as much if not more. In fact, I expend as much energy on internal as on external communications. I never assume anymore that even my closest associates can read my mind—I've learned too much watching false information spread.[4]

Once a vision is cast, it may need to be cast again—several times. Since God's vision always surpasses human comprehension, it requires persistence on the part of leaders to make sure everyone catches it and remembers it. Ultimately, God's vision must be transmitted by the Spirit of God. This principle was demonstrated in the Old Testament. When the Arameans tried to capture the prophet Elisha, his servant despaired, saying, "Oh, my lord, what shall we do?" (2 Kings 6:15). Elisha's response communicated a vision of God's control over the situation:

> "Don't be afraid," the prophet answered. "Those who
> are with us are more than those who are with
> them."
> And Elisha prayed, "O LORD, open his eyes so he
> may see." Then the LORD opened the servant's eyes,
> and he looked and saw the hills full of horses and
> chariots of fire all around Elisha. (2 Kings 6:16–17)

Paul expanded on this principle in his writings to the church at Corinth. "The man without the Spirit does not accept the things that come from the Spirit of God, for they are foolishness to him, and he cannot understand them, because they are spiritually discerned" (1 Corinthians 2:14); "The god of this age has blinded the minds of unbelievers, so that they cannot see the light of the gospel of the glory of Christ, who is the image of God" (2 Corinthians 4:4). The implications of the life of Christ will be lost to unbelievers apart from the convicting work of the Holy Spirit.

But for those of us who have the Holy Spirit living in us, we are called to be kingdom builders who play an active role in the realization of God's vision. Through mentoring relationships, we enlist others in this grand scheme of redemption that God planned out before the foundations of the world were set. We recruit men and women to participate in a vision that will have eternal ramifications, eternal consequences. It is the longing of all human hearts to participate in something that will outlive them.

Casting the Vision at Home

It is one thing to have vision; it is quite another to communicate that vision to others to enable them to embrace it and internalize it. Those who follow Christ are commissioned to communicate the vision of newness of life to others within their spheres of influence. The obvious place for this communication to start is in the home with our own children. In his book *Visioneering,* Andy Stanley writes:

> The most significant visions are not cast by great orators from a stage. They are cast at the bedsides of our children. The greatest vision-casting opportunities happen between the hours of 7:30 and 9:30 p.m. Monday through Sunday. In these closing hours of the day we have a unique opportunity to plant the seeds of what could be and what should be. Take advantage of every opportunity you get.[5]

The central biblical passage concerning parents' responsibility to create an environment in which their children will hear and embrace the teachings and principles of Scripture is the great Hebrew *shema* of Deuteronomy 6:4–9:

> Hear, O Israel: The LORD our God, the LORD is one. Love the LORD your God with all your heart and with all your soul and with all your strength. These commandments that I give you today are to be upon your hearts. Impress them on your children. Talk about them when you sit at home and when you walk along the road, when you lie down and when you get up. Tie them as symbols on your hands and bind them on your foreheads. Write them on the doorframes of your houses and on your gates.

Because people cannot give away what they do not possess, it is first necessary that parents know and love the Lord before they can hope to instill spiritual truth in the hearts of the next generation. Only those who love the Lord themselves will be effective in passing on this love to others. Many people were raised by parents who did not love God in an all-encompassing way. There was a great disparity between what the parents said they wanted their children to do and the way they actually lived their own lives. Such parents use the classic statement, "Do as I say, not as I do." There is something inherently wrong about that situation. Such a lack of integrity undermines people's ability to communicate their vision in a way that will infect others. Communication involves more than words. It involves *logos* (words and concepts), *ethos* (behavior and character), and *pathos* (passion and sympathy). Clear communication is borne of what we say, what we do, and who we are. There must be integrity and alignment in order for our communication to be credible and persuasive.

Many parents have discovered the futility of trying to raise their children to have moral standards they themselves do not possess. It is pointless to try to get children to obey God without loving him, and it is impossible for parents to teach their children to love God if they themselves do not.

This passage also underscores the fact that vision is imparted in both formal and informal ways. In these verses, parents are told to impress God's commandments on their children not only in more structured settings ("when you sit at home," v. 7), but also in unstructured and spontaneous ways ("when you walk along the road," v. 7). When people are serious about knowing God, they begin to incarnate and exhibit what they speak. Spiritual and moral principles are best conveyed in the laboratory of life; they are conveyed as much through character as they are through words. Truth is most effectively proclaimed through the consistency of words and work.

The message of Proverbs 2 is that wisdom can be found only if it is sought intentionally:

> My son, if you accept my words and store up my
> commands within you, turning your ear to wisdom
> and applying your heart to understanding, and if you
> call out for insight and cry aloud for understanding,
> and if you look for it as for silver and search for it as
> for hidden treasure, then you will understand the
> fear of the LORD and find the knowledge of God.
> (Proverbs 2:1–5)

The reason this father could implore his son to pursue wisdom is that the son had seen the father do the same. Parents who try to instruct their children to fear the Lord without fearing the Lord themselves are like those who try to describe something they haven't seen. Larry Crabb expands upon the power and importance of casting a vision for another person:

> What would it be like if we had a vision for each
> other, if we could see the lost glory in ourselves, our
> family, and our friends? What would the effect on
> your sons and daughters be if they realized that you
> were caught up with the possibilities of restored
> glory, of what they could become—not successful,
> talented, good looking, or rich but kind, strong and
> self-assured, fully alive.
>
> When people connect with each other on the basis
> of a vision for who they are and what they could
> become; when we see in others what little of Jesus has
> already begun to form beneath the insecurity, fear and
> pride; when we long beyond anything else to see that
> little bit of Jesus develop and mature; then something
> is released from within us that has the power to form
> more of Jesus within them. That power is the life of
> Christ, carried into another soul across the bridge of
> our vision for them, a life that touches the life in
> another with nourishing power. Vision for others both
> bridges the distance between two souls and triggers
> the release of the power within us.[6]

CASTING GOD'S VISION

When God provided David with a vision of the Jerusalem temple, the king wanted to be personally instrumental in making that dream a reality. But the Lord told David that the job of building the temple would be given to Solomon, David's son and successor. David chose not to view himself as having been cut out of the action. Instead, he energetically undertook his new charge—that of instilling his vision and passion for the temple in Solomon and enlisting his unqualified support:

King David rose to his feet and said: "Listen to me, my brothers and my people. I had it in my heart to build a house as a place of rest for the ark of the covenant of the LORD, for the footstool of our God, and I made plans to build it. But God said to me, 'You are not to build a house for my Name, because you are a warrior and have shed blood.' ...

"He said to me: 'Solomon your son is the one who will build my house and my courts, for I have chosen him to be my son, and I will be his father. I will establish his kingdom forever if he is unswerving in carrying out my commands and laws, as is being done at this time.'

"So now I charge you in the sight of all Israel and of the assembly of the LORD, and in the hearing of our God: Be careful to follow all the commands of the LORD your God, that you may possess this good land and pass it on as an inheritance to your descendants forever.

"And you, my son Solomon, acknowledge the God of your father, and serve him with wholehearted devotion and with a willing mind, for the LORD searches every heart and understands every motive behind the thoughts. If you seek him, he will be found by you; but if you forsake him, he will reject you forever. Consider now, for the LORD has chosen you to build a temple as a sanctuary. Be strong and do the work."

Then David gave his son Solomon the plans for the portico of the temple, its buildings, its storerooms, its upper parts, its inner rooms and the place of atonement. He gave him the plans of all that the Spirit had put in his mind for the courts of the temple of the LORD and all the surrounding rooms, for the treasuries of the temple of God and for the treasuries for the dedicated things.... He also gave him the plan for the chariot, that is, the cherubim of gold that spread their wings and shelter the ark of the covenant of the LORD.

"All this," David said, "I have in writing from the hand of the LORD upon me, and he gave me understanding in all the details of the plan."

David also said to Solomon his son, "Be strong and courageous, and do the work. Do not be afraid or discouraged, for the LORD God, my God, is with you. He will not fail you or forsake you until all the work for the service of the temple of the LORD is finished. The divisions of the priests and Levites are ready for all the work on the temple of God, and every willing man skilled in any craft will help you in all the work. The officials and all the people will obey your every command." (1 Chronicles 28:2–3, 6–12, 18–21)

Notice how David proceeded. First, he made it clear that the vision had come from God (vv. 2–3). Second, he informed Solomon that his role would be to lead the charge in building the temple (vv. 6–7). Such a task would require total devotion to the Lord and to the work—a halfhearted effort wouldn't get the job done (vv. 8–10). Third, David assured the people that this enormous task would be accomplished because God would enable Solomon to get the job done (v. 6). Fourth, David gave his son sufficient detail about the temple that Solomon could visualize what it would look like (vv. 11–19). Finally, after casting the vision, the king gave his son another dose of encouragement (vv. 20–21). David actively participated in preparing his successor. He passed the baton to his son publicly and privately by endowing him with the vision for the temple. One of the most significant tasks of a leader is to transmit the organizational vision to others.

How Sweet It Is!

Steve always dreamed of owning his own business, but more than that, Steve truly believed in his dream to put affordable computers in every home and office. He really believed that it would revolutionize the world. So he took the plunge and started his own computer company. The only problem was that he knew computers; he didn't know business. He needed the best CEO he could get, and that meant John Sculley, CEO of PepsiCo. Inc. Somehow Steve had to convince Sculley to leave his prominent position at one of the most prestigious and profitable companies in the world and run Steve's fledgling company.

Somehow, some way, Steve managed to schedule a meeting with John Sculley. Sculley listened patiently to the young man's presentation. He even allowed Steve to schedule another meeting. Finally, after several appointments, Sculley introduced Steve to reality: "You'd have to give me a million-dollar salary, a million-dollar signing bonus, and a million-dollar severance package."

Steve was shocked. He couldn't afford anything close to those figures. Still, his boldness and passion blurted words out of his mouth: "You've got it. Even if I have to pay for it out of my own pocket."

Sculley didn't become CEO of a multinational corporation by being foolish. He knew a bluff when he heard one. "Steve, I'd love to be an adviser, but I don't think I can come as CEO."

Steve dropped his head, took a long breath, and issued a challenge that pierced Sculley to the core. Looking him right in the eye, Steve simply asked, "Do you want to spend the rest of your life selling sugared water, or do you want a chance to change the world?" John Sculley resigned from PepsiCo and took Steve Jobs up on his offer to lead a fledgling computer company called Apple. And together they really did change the world.[7]

God placed in each of us a yearning for significance. Yet few of us actually devote our lives to great endeavors. The message of Christianity tells us that we can participate in something that stretches beyond our brief lives on earth. By passing on the vision of God to the next generation of his people, we can have a hand in eternity.

1. Clifton Fadiman, ed., *The Little, Brown Book of Anecdotes* (Boston: Little, Brown, and Company, 1985), 548.
2. Leonard Sweet, *Aqua Church* (Loveland, CO: Group Publishing, 1999), 167.
3. James Emery White, *Life-Defining Moments* (Colorado Springs: WaterBrook Press, 2001), 69.
4. Hans Finzel, *The Top Ten Mistakes Leaders Make* (Colorado Springs: Victor Books, 2000), 115.
5. Andy Stanley, *Visioneering* (Sisters, OR: Multnomah, 1999), 114.
6. Larry Crabb, *Connecting* (Nashville: Word, 1997), 65.
7. Adapted from John Sculley, *Odyssey* (New York: Harper & Row, 1987), 56–91.

CHAPTER 8

Innovation

CHANGE IS NORMAL

A cartoon I saw in *The New Yorker* showed a CEO winding up his speech at a board meeting with the following sentence: "And so, while the end-of-the-world scenario will be rife with unimaginable horrors, we believe that the pre-end period will be filled with unprecedented opportunities for profit."[1] Somehow that seems to capture the spirit of our times.

Many of us live with the same perspective as King Hezekiah in 2 Kings 20:19. After being told by the prophet Isaiah that, because of his pride and arrogance, his wealth and posterity would fall into the hands of the Babylonians, he actually said, "The word of the LORD that you have spoken is good." He said this was because he thought, "Will there not be peace and security in my lifetime?" Hezekiah was only concerned with how things would be during his own time here on earth. He gave no thought to the hardships others would endure after he was gone. Many of our environmental and financial decisions demonstrate this same outlook. And yet our time on earth is only a speck in cosmic terms. A. W. Tozer rightly said,

> The days of the years of our lives are few, and swifter than a weaver's shuttle. Life is a short and fevered

> rehearsal for a concert we cannot stay to give. Just
> when we appear to have gained some proficiency, we
> are forced to lay our instruments down. There is sim-
> ply not time enough to think, to become, to perform
> what the constitution of our natures indicates we are
> capable of.[2]

If life here on earth is all there is, then our mortality is dis-
tressing. But the Bible invites us to see that there is more to this
life than the constant pendulum swing from happiness to regret.
We are not defined by our past; we are defined by our future.
We have a destiny, a hope, and a future. The past is finite, but
the future is unbounded. The past is fixed, but lasting change is
possible for those of us who are united with the God who makes
all things new (Revelation 21:5). In fact, change is not only possible, it is normative for those of us who live our lives with a
sense of holy calling, a determination to follow Jesus wherever
he leads.

JESUS, THE CHANGE AGENT

An old story has a husband asking his wife, "Honey, why do
you cut off the ends of a roast before you cook it?"

"Because my mother did it that way," she responded with a
smile.

Curious, the husband called the wife's mother and asked her
the same question. When she gave an identical answer, he called
his wife's grandmother. The moment the elderly matron heard
the question she laughed and said, "I don't know why *they* cut
off the ends of the roast, but I did it that way because a full roast
wouldn't fit in my pan."

That story illustrates how most practices are initiated to
serve a purpose. But over time, even the best practice can lose
its usefulness. It takes a wise leader to know when to change
something. It takes insight to recognize when it is time for

innovation. Jesus certainly understood the role of change and rebuked those who stood in the way of innovation:

> Now John's disciples and the Pharisees were fasting. Some people came and asked Jesus, "How is it that John's disciples and the disciples of the Pharisees are fasting, but yours are not?"
>
> Jesus answered, "How can the guests of the bridegroom fast while he is with them? They cannot, so long as they have him with them. But the time will come when the bridegroom will be taken from them, and on that day they will fast.
>
> "No one sews a patch of unshrunk cloth on an old garment. If he does, the new piece will pull away from the old, making the tear worse. And no one pours new wine into old wineskins. If he does, the wine will burst the skins, and both the wine and the wineskins will be ruined. No, he pours new wine into new wineskins." (Mark 2:18–22)

The Pharisees chided Jesus because he didn't force his disciples to fast. Jesus informed them that he had not come to add a few new rules and regulations to Judaism. He had something entirely new to impart. The Lord made it clear to those religious leaders that he hadn't come to patch an old system. Such an effort would be as foolish as putting a patch of unshrunk cloth on an old garment, or putting new wine in an old wineskin. When the patch shrank, the garment would tear. When the wine fermented, the wineskin would burst. The old forms of Judaism could never contain the spirit of Jesus' message.

Change challenges our existing categories. In order to change we must reorder our thought processes and see the same things in new ways. The idea that the Messiah would suffer and serve and live in poverty and humility—that was unthinkable for Jewish people prior to the incarnation. They would never have imagined that the Messiah would be born in obscurity and die a criminal's death. This concept was out of their range of thought. Jesus was an innovator, a change agent. So is every effective leader.

Change on a Cosmic Scale

In one way or another, all of us have an aversion to change, especially when things appear to be going reasonably well. But we serve a God who makes all things new (Revelation 21:5). God is not interested in preserving the status quo; he is committed to nothing less than inaugurating an entirely new order of creation. The incarnation of God the Son brought about a radical change that disrupted the status quo for all eternity. The gospel of John begins:

> In the beginning was the Word, and the Word was with God, and the Word was God. He was with God in the beginning.
>
> Through him all things were made; without him nothing was made that has been made. In him was life, and that life was the light of men. The light shines in the darkness, but the darkness has not understood it.
>
> There came a man who was sent from God; his name was John. He came as a witness to testify concerning that light, so that through him all men might believe. He himself was not the light; he came only as a witness to the light. The true light that gives light to every man was coming into the world.
>
> He was in the world, and though the world was made through him, the world did not recognize him. He came to that which was his own, but his own did not receive him. Yet to all who received him, to those who believed in his name, he gave the right to become children of God—children born not of natural descent, nor of human decision or a husband's will, but born of God.

> The Word became flesh and made his dwelling among us. We have seen his glory, the glory of the One and Only, who came from the Father, full of grace and truth. John testifies concerning him. He cries out, saying, "This was he of whom I said, 'He who comes after me has surpassed me because he was before me.'" From the fullness of his grace we have all received one blessing after another. For the law was given through Moses; grace and truth came through Jesus Christ. No one has ever seen God, but God the One and Only, who is at the Father's side, has made him known. (John 1:1–18)

John deliberately opened his gospel with an allusion to the opening words of the creation account in Genesis 1. Actually, John goes back before Genesis 1, which talks about the beginning of creation. Even before creation, the Word existed. At the time of the beginning, the Word already *was*. Through the mystery of the incarnation, the Word who created the world entered into his own creation and became one of us. He who forever existed as spirit has now and for all eternity become the God-man. There is a man in heaven—Christ is now in his glorified resurrection body—and because of this change, he has made it possible for us to enter into the intimacy of fellowship with God himself. "Father, I want those you have given me to be with me where I am, and to see my glory, the glory you have given me because you loved me before the creation of the world" (John 17:24).

Significantly, the world he created is complex and elegant—filled with clues about the character and nature of its creator. The more we learn about this created order, the more sophisticated its designer appears. The magnificent design of the solar system and all the many galaxies we are now able to observe make it clear just how creative the creator must be. But we need not limit our observations to a telescope. By looking through a microscope, the same variety and imagination can be seen. From the very large to the very small, God's intricate design reveals him to be a creator of amazing innovation and diversity.

It should not be surprising, then, that the One who infused creation with change and innovation should himself be innovative in his dealings with human beings. The flood, the call of Abraham, the Mosaic covenant, the new covenant, the incarnation, the crucifixion, the resurrection, the day of Pentecost, the second advent, the new heavens and new earth—all of these illustrate the dramatic and unprecedented innovations that have been wrought by God.

The apostle Paul picked up this theme when he wrote:

> For Christ's love compels us, because we are convinced that one died for all, and therefore all died. And he died for all, that those who live should no longer live for themselves but for him who died for them and was raised again.
>
> So from now on we regard no one from a worldly point of view. Though we once regarded Christ in this way, we do so no longer. *Therefore, if anyone is in Christ, he is a new creation; the old has gone, the new has come!* All this is from God, who reconciled us to himself through Christ and gave us the ministry of reconciliation: that God was reconciling the world to himself in Christ, not counting men's sins against them. And he has committed to us the message of reconciliation. We are therefore Christ's ambassadors, as though God were making his appeal through us. We implore you on Christ's behalf: Be reconciled to God. God made him who had no sin to be sin for us, so that in him we might become the righteousness of God. (2 Corinthians 5:14–21)

Here is the most inventive mind of all, taking on human flesh and limitations. He did that so that you and I can enjoy intimacy with him. As we grow in him we are being made truly human. Through his transforming power, we become the people God intended us to be. James S. Steward, noted Scottish preacher and friend of the famous William Barclay, tells us there once was in the city of Florence a massive, shapeless block of marble that seemed fitted to be the raw material of some colossal statue. One sculptor after another tried his hand at it, without success. They cut and carved and hewed and chipped at it, until it seemed hopelessly disfigured.

Then someone suggested they give Michelangelo a shot at it. He began by having a house built right over the block of marble, and for long months he was shut up there with it, nobody knowing what he was doing. Then one day he flung open the door and told everyone to come in. They did, and there before their eyes—instead of a shapeless, meaningless block of marble—was the magnificent statue of David, one of the glories of the world. So it is that Christ takes defeated and disfigured lives and refashions them, changing them into the very image of God.[3]

No other religion has a concept such as this one. In every other religious system, men and women are left to save themselves. To paraphrase Larry Hall, we are left to lift ourselves off the ground by our own shirt collar.[4] Only the Bible shows us a true assessment of the human condition. Only here do we see our great dignity and our great depravity. Because we see ourselves honestly and accurately, we understand that God had to reach down in order to lift us up. Luder Whitlock, former president of Reformed Theological Seminary, writes:

> The gospel offers an escape from the deadening influence of sin that chokes the joy from life and dashes it to the ground, producing an ugly, broken mess. God converts the believer into a new person in Christ. As the Lord remakes that person in his image, he gives the believer a new ability to reshape life and the world into a thing of beauty reflective of God's own nature. The innovative, aesthetic

dimensions of life find redemptive stimulation, and
the corrosive, destructive tendency of sinful influence gradually diminishes as spiritual maturity
increases. As the Bible states, "He has made everything beautiful in its time" (Ecclesiastes 3:11). This
is true of God's transforming influence on
Christians. God's perfection is linked to his beauty,
so as sin and its influence diminish, his beauty is
manifested, though imperfectly, in us. God's creativity resulted in the making of not only new things
but beautiful things. In similar fashion, as we
become more like God, we become not only innovative or creative, but we develop a love for beauty
and a desire to multiply it.[5]

The biblical doctrine of grace elevates without inflating; it
humbles without degrading. We can repair and renovate, we
can make things *like* new, but only God can make things new.

THE NECESSITY OF CHANGE

Change and innovation are integral components of both bio-
logical and spiritual growth. The Scriptures focus more on
process than on product, because all believers are in a process
(whether we resist it or not) of becoming the people God meant
us to be. Without change, growth is impossible. Abram learned
the truth that it is impossible to stay where one is and go with
God at the same time:

The LORD had said to Abram, "Leave your country,
your people and your father's household and go to
the land I will show you.
"I will make you into a great nation and I will
bless you; I will make your name great, and you will
be a blessing. I will bless those who bless you, and

whoever curses you I will curse; and all peoples on
earth will be blessed through you." (Genesis 12:1–3)

Abram was well established in Ur of the Chaldeans when
God called him to leave his homeland. After he had settled for
some time in Haran, his father Terah died, and the Lord once
again instructed Abram to uproot himself, this time at the age of
seventy-five. Since the flood, God had been working with the
nations in general, but now he was selecting a man whose
descendants would constitute a new people who would be set
apart for him. The Abrahamic covenant became the vehicle
through which God would bless "all peoples on earth," since the
Messiah would come from the seed of Abram.

Abram experienced immense change through his encounters with God. This is no mere shifting of external elements in
his life, not simply an adjustment of activity or schedule. God
asked for a complete overhaul of Abram's career, dreams, and
destiny. God even changed his name from Abram to Abraham to
signify the depth of this change. But there was a huge gap
between the time when the promise was given and the time
when it was fulfilled. Weeks turned into months, months turned
into years, and years turned into decades—and still Abraham
and Sarah had no child.

How did Abraham respond? Very simply, "Abram believed
the LORD" (Genesis 15:6). Abraham trusted God in spite of the
evidence to the contrary. He continued to walk in obedience and
faith. Then, when it seemed completely impossible, and
Abraham acknowledged his inability to provide an heir for himself, God provided.

When God calls, it requires trust and obedience to follow
him. It is not simply a call to a new *way* of life; it is a call to a new
kind of life. This level of uprooting and total change can generate
great stress. It is threatening, scary, and difficult. Change of this
magnitude must be deeply rooted in a solid core of values.

When we as leaders contemplate change, our first consider-
ation must be the anchors that provide stability in a changing

environment. Abraham believed in the Lord, and that security allowed him to pursue revolutionary change. Similarly, the Christian life is an ongoing process of change and internal revolution, grounded in the belief that this process is reforming those of us who participate in it to become more Christlike.

This process should not be thought of as "pain free." God invites us to do something counterintuitive: to go through the pain and not around it. God often uses the painful experiences of life to shape us and to aid the transformation process. Jim McGuiggan writes:

> When we say suffering and death can be redemptive, we're not saying they're not hateful or excruciating; we're not saying the sufferers aren't in agony. No! We're speaking our faith that God will not allow us to face *anything* without the privilege of his working it for good—if we will but say yes to his offer. He will not allow suffering to be meaningless but will, with our permission, force it to be the soil out of which things like compassion, sympathy, courage, and service grow.[6]

To take what Shakespeare called "the slings and arrows of outrageous fortune"[7] and weave them into a beautiful tapestry takes imagination, creativity, and innovation of the highest level. Our Creator-God promises to redeem our pain and refine us in the process.

Imagine the opportunity that is available to us—to spend all of eternity in unbroken fellowship with this level of innovation! Heaven will not be static. Nothing can remain the same in his presence. God is always full of wonderful surprises. The variety we observe on earth and in the cosmos is a mere shadow of the way things will be in heaven. Whatever adventures this life allows us, whatever joys and excitements we feel here, will pale in comparison to those we will experience in heaven.

So God invites us to go through his refining process and

promises us that he will be on the other end of it. He will receive us and welcome us to a place beyond our wildest imagination. The apostle Paul knew this truth well and wrote, "I consider that our present sufferings are not worth comparing with the glory that will be revealed in us" (Romans 8:18).

Managing Change

Change is part of God's plan for us, but it is still hard. Change is tough enough when we are the only ones involved. But the role of a leader is to bring about change in others and/or in an organization. Now that is *really* tough! God modeled some powerful principles of organizational change when he urged the exclusively Jewish church in Jerusalem to embrace Gentiles. In Acts 10 Luke tells the story:

> About noon the following day as [Cornelius's servants] were on their journey and approaching the city, Peter went up on the roof to pray. He became hungry and wanted something to eat, and while the meal was being prepared, he fell into a trance. He saw heaven opened and something like a large sheet being let down to earth by its four corners. It contained all kinds of four-footed animals, as well as reptiles of the earth and birds of the air. Then a voice told him, "Get up, Peter. Kill and eat."
>
> "Surely not, Lord!" Peter replied. "I have never eaten anything impure or unclean."
>
> The voice spoke to him a second time, "Do not call anything impure that God has made clean."
>
> This happened three times, and immediately the sheet was taken back to heaven.
>
> While Peter was wondering about the meaning of the vision, the men sent by Cornelius found out where Simon's house was and stopped at the gate. They called out, asking if Simon who was known as Peter was staying there.

While Peter was still thinking about the vision, the Spirit said to him, "Simon, three men are looking for you. So get up and go downstairs. Do not hesitate to go with them, for I have sent them."

Peter went down and said to the men, "I'm the one you're looking for. Why have you come?"

The men replied, "We have come from Cornelius the centurion. He is a righteous and God-fearing man, who is respected by all the Jewish people. A holy angel told him to have you come to his house so that he could hear what you have to say." Then Peter invited the men into the house to be his guests.

The next day Peter started out with them, and some of the brothers from Joppa went along. The following day he arrived in Caesarea. Cornelius was expecting them and had called together his relatives and close friends. As Peter entered the house, Cornelius met him and fell at his feet in reverence. But Peter made him get up. "Stand up," he said, "I am only a man myself."

Talking with him, Peter went inside and found a large gathering of people. He said to them: "You are well aware that it is against our law for a Jew to associate with a Gentile or visit him. But God has shown me that I should not call any man impure or unclean…. I now realize how true it is that God does not show favoritism but accepts men from every nation who fear him and do what is right." (Acts 10:9–28, 34–35)

Change is inherent in leadership. The enormous reversal described in this passage shows how God led Peter from being an opponent of change to becoming its champion. Notice seven principles from the passage:

■ God started where Peter was. He addressed Peter's values and convictions (vv. 9–16). The wise innovator takes time to understand the people who must adapt to the change and demonstrates that it will not violate their values and convictions (v. 15).

■ God allowed Peter to challenge the idea (vv. 14–15). If people's objections aren't dealt with in a forthright and honest manner, the leader can begin to perceive their concerns as antagonism.

■ God gave Peter time to work through his resistance (vv. 16–17). Adaptation to change takes time, and the wise leader allows people the needed time to work through their reservations.

■ God permitted Peter to observe change in a limited situation before suggesting wholesale change. He allowed Peter to "try on" the change under controlled circumstances (vv. 18–23). Effective leaders allow their people to experiment with the process of change in order for them to begin to anticipate its effects.

■ God saw that the change proposal was well prepared (vv. 1–7, 19–23, 30–33). God anticipated Peter's questions and had evidence ready to support his answers. When introducing change, wise leaders will be prepared to answer questions that might arise.

■ God didn't ask Peter to "change"; he invited him to participate in improving what Peter loved. Peter quickly saw the advantage of the new over the old (v. 34). Early in the process, God demonstrated the benefits that the "new" would produce (vv. 44–46). Abandoning the comfort of the status quo can be threatening, and understanding leaders will help their followers to recognize the improvements the change will bring about.

■ God convinced a key leader and allowed that leader

himself to champion the change (Acts 11:1–18). Individuals are easier to work with than a group. Some changes need the support of a few key leaders who will then help others to reconcile themselves to the new circumstances.

CHANGING AND STAYING THE SAME—AT THE SAME TIME?

Change is important. But it is also important to cling to core values. Peter experienced that tension, and God helped him facilitate change while not abandoning his core values. James C. Collins and Jerry I. Porras help us to understand the importance of both change and core values to a leader. In their excellent book *Built to Last*, they note that once a visionary company identifies its core ideology, it preserves it almost religiously—changing it seldom, if ever. They conclude:

> [C]ore values in a visionary company form a rock-solid foundation and do not drift with the trends and fashions of the day. In some cases, the core values have remained intact for well over one hundred years.... Yet, while keeping their core ideologies tightly fixed, visionary companies display a powerful desire for progress that enables them to change and adapt without compromising their cherished core ideals.[8]

Collins and Porras effectively make the point that capable leaders, who recognize their core values, can change practices and procedures to enable their organization to move forward.

Acts 16 is a record of a portion of Paul's missionary travels. He was not one to be haphazard in his planning, but he remained open to the leadership of his Lord:

> Paul and his companions traveled throughout the region of Phrygia and Galatia, having been kept by

the Holy Spirit from preaching the word in the
province of Asia. When they came to the border of
Mysia, they tried to enter Bithynia, but the Spirit of
Jesus would not allow them to. So they passed by
Mysia and went down to Troas. During the night Paul
had a vision of a man of Macedonia standing and beg-
ging him, "Come over to Macedonia and help us."
After Paul had seen the vision, we got ready at once
to leave for Macedonia, concluding that God had
called us to preach the gospel to them. (Acts 16:6–10)

Paul had his itinerary and his maps. In modern terms, we
would say that "Bithynia or Bust" was written on the side of his
chariot. But God changed this imaginary slogan to "Macedonia
or Bust!" Change—new direction. But Paul's core value was not
Bithynia. It was fulfilling God's desire to expand his kingdom.
Because he didn't confuse his desire (to go to Bithynia) with his
core value (to follow God's call), Paul enthusiastically "sailed
straight for Samothrace [in the Greek province of Macedonia]"
(v. 11). Like Paul, all godly leaders need the ability to hold to
core values while making those changes necessary to advance
their cause.

Leonard Sweet is the dean of the theological school and vice
president at Drew University in Madison, New Jersey. He has
written extensively to church leaders about the need to distin-
guish between content and containers. In his book *Aqua Church*,
he writes,

Water is a liquid that fills the shape of any receptacle.
As long as we trust the water and don't tamper with
the recipe—don't dilute it, thicken it, or separate its
ingredients—the content can remain the same while
containers change…. I am a virtual fundamentalist
about content. I am a virtual libertarian about containers. Only in Jesus the Christ did the container
and content become one. Jesus' comments about
new wine in old wineskins remind us that we cannot

make an idolatry of any form or container. We must
not elevate an ecclesial form to the level of authority
or primacy that belongs only to the content.... The
mystery of the gospel is this: It is always the same
(content), and it is always changing (containers). In
fact, for the gospel to remain the same, it has to
change.... In fact, one of the ways you know the old,
old truths are true is their ability to assume amazing
and unfamiliar shapes while remaining themselves
and without compromising their integrity.[9]

One of the great hymns of the church says, "God is the fountain whence ten thousand blessings flow." God is a fountain. St.
Gregory of Nyssa used this imagery when he wrote:

If anyone happened to be near the fountain which
Scripture says rose from the earth at the beginning of
creation ... he would approach it marveling at the
endless stream of water gushing forth and bubbling
out. Never could he say that he had seen all the
water.... In the same way, the person looking at the
divine, invisible beauty will always discover it anew
since he will see it as something newer and more
wondrous in comparison to what he had already
comprehended.[10]

A fountain is still, yet it moves, constant and ever-changing,
quiet and savage. It welcomes and warns. It goes up and down,
in and out all at the same time. It is water, but not the way most
of us normally think of water. Innovative and faithful simulta-
neously, just like God, just like godly leaders.

1. Robert Mankoff, *The New Yorker,* September 9, 2002.
2. A. W. Tozer, *The Knowledge of the Holy* (New York: Harper & Row,
   1961), 52.

3. James S. Steward, *The Gates of New Life* (Edinburgh: T&T Clark, 1937), 245–46.

4. Larry E. Hall, *No Longer I* (Abilene, TX: ACU Press, 1998), 127.

5. Luder G. Whitlock Jr., *The Spiritual Quest* (Grand Rapids, MI: Baker Books, 2000), 148–49.

6. Jim McGuiggan, *The God of the Towel* (West Monroe, LA: Howard Publishing Company, 1997), 178.

7. *Hamlet*, act 3, scene 1, line 59.

8. James C. Collins and Jerry I. Porras, *Built to Last* (New York: Harper Business, 1997), 8–9.

9. Leonard Sweet, *Aqua Church* (Loveland, CO: Group Publishing, 1999), 28–30.

10. St. Gregory of Nyssa, *Commentary on the Song of Songs* (Brookline, MA: Hellenic College Press, 1987), 201.

CHAPTER 9

Decision Making

DECISION MAKING REQUIRES CORRECT THINKING

There is a thought-provoking scene in Lewis Carroll's classic children's tale, *Alice's Adventures in Wonderland*. Young Alice comes to a fork in the road and asks the Cheshire Cat which direction she should take. "'That depends a good deal on where you want to get to,' said the Cat.

"'I don't much care where—' said Alice.

"'Then it doesn't matter which way you walk,' said the Cat."[1]

Life is filled with decisions, many of which never even reach our conscious level. Which socks to wear? Should the shirt be buttoned from the top down or from the bottom up? Which lane to drive in? Most of these decisions are made out of habit.

On the other hand, there are some decisions that we spend time thinking about. What sounds good for lunch? Which voice mail needs to be answered first? Can the haircut wait until next week? These decisions may seem small and insignificant, but woven together, they form the tapestry of our daily lives.

Then there are life-altering decisions that cause us to struggle. Which career path is most in line with our unique skill sets and calling? Should we marry or remain single? Which church will allow us the best opportunity to grow and minister to others? These are often hard choices that deserve a great amount of thought.

Often the same decision-making process we use for minor issues is used for major decisions as well. So the question is: How do we choose wisely? What criteria do we use to evaluate, to discern the best course of action? Clearly, gathering information and carefully analyzing our options is essential. Beyond that, we need wisdom and clarity of thought in order to make prudent decisions based on the facts at hand and our understanding of God's will.

Many bad choices are made simply because we move through the decision-making process too hastily, basing our conclusions on emotions, bad information, or impulses. There is something to be said for "gut reactions," but basing our every purchase on our feelings would lead to a lot of buyer's remorse. The opposite extreme would be to automatically rule out any emotional factors in our decision-making method. We should allow an inner sense of conviction to serve as a "red flag," without allowing ourselves to fall into the "paralysis of analysis" when it comes to determining our next move.

The complexity of this issue shows how important it is not to make decisions in a vacuum. Particularly on very important matters, it is wise to seek counsel and advice from others who are experienced and godly. The only basis for really good decisions is correct thinking. This kind of wisdom comes from above and is given to us through four primary avenues—God's Word, God's Spirit, God's providence, and God's people. In other words, to ensure good decision-making habits, we must be people whose minds are consistently being renewed by God's Word. We must also be people who walk in step with the Spirit of God, paying attention to his promptings and leadings. We must watch carefully and understand how God works providentially in our circumstances. And we must live in community with other faithful believers.

THE POWER OF PRAYER

God is sovereign—at times, inscrutably so. That being the case, in what sense can we say that the sovereign Lord, the One who transcends all imaginable boundaries and who knows all things, makes decisions? In his timeless plan, God has conceived all possible scenarios and has thought of every possible contingency. There has never been an event that took God by surprise, and there never will be.

There is great comfort in this knowledge, because we come to realize that as imperfect creatures living in an imperfect world, we can never really disappoint God. We can grieve him, but we cannot thwart or frustrate him. In spite of how our world appears to us, because of God's supreme sovereignty and wisdom, it is exactly the way he knew it would be, and we are right on schedule in the unfolding of his plan to bring us to the best of all possible worlds. God has even incorporated the foolish, sinful decisions of people into his divine scheme. Things that were meant for evil and harmful purposes, God weaves into his good will to accomplish his program in our world (Genesis 50:20). Because he is omniscient, his plan is based not on appearances but on consequences. Because he is omnipotent, he is fully able to accomplish his purposes. Because he is omnipresent, his dominion continually encompasses the created order. Because he is not bound by space and time, he views all things from the perspective of an eternal *now*; a particular moment to us can be an eternity to God, and yet the entire life span of the cosmos can be an instant to him (2 Peter 3:8).

Though the Lord our God sits enthroned on high, he "stoops down to look on the heavens and the earth" (Psalm 113:6). He is transcendent and majestic, but he is also immanent, attentive, and compassionate. Even though God is all-powerful, all-knowing, and ever-present, the Scriptures portray his very real interaction with his people in earthly time and space and affirm that our prayers make a difference in the outworking of God's purposes. As Philip Yancey writes:

God is not a blurry power living somewhere in the
sky, not an abstraction like the Greeks proposed, not
a sensual super-human like the Romans worshiped,
and definitely not the absentee watchmaker of the
Deists. God is *personal*. He enters into people's lives,
messes with families, calls people to account. Most of
all, God loves.[2]

God is not a man, nor does he change his mind (1 Samuel
15:29). However, the Bible does not shrink from attributing
emotions to him. No one has expressed this fact more eloquently than Jewish theologian Abraham Heschel:

To the prophet, God does not reveal himself in an
abstract absoluteness, but in a personal and intimate
relation to the world. He does not simply command
and expect obedience; He is also moved and affected
by what happens in the world, and reacts accord-
ingly. Events and human actions rouse in him joy or
sorrow, pleasure or wrath.... Man's deeds may move
Him, affect Him, grieve Him or, on the other hand,
gladden and please Him.

The God of Israel is a God Who loves, a God Who
is known to, and concerned with, man. He not only
rules the world in the majesty of his might and wisdom, but reacts intimately to the events of history.[3]

Of course, before God was the God of Israel, he was the God
of Abraham. The story of Abraham's prayers on behalf of the
few righteous people in Sodom illustrates the biblical truth that
God mysteriously incorporates our prayers into his eternal plan.
Abraham founded his intercession on the unswerving justice of
the Ruler of the world:

Then the LORD said, "The outcry against Sodom and
Gomorrah is so great and their sin so grievous that I
will go down and see if what they have done is as

bad as the outcry that has reached me. If not, I will know."

The men turned away and went toward Sodom, but Abraham remained standing before the LORD. Then Abraham approached him and said: "Will you sweep away the righteous with the wicked? What if there are fifty righteous people in the city? Will you really sweep it away and not spare the place for the sake of the fifty righteous people in it? Far be it from you to do such a thing—to kill the righteous with the wicked, treating the righteous and the wicked alike. Far be it from you! Will not the Judge of all the earth do right?"

The LORD said, "If I find fifty righteous people in the city of Sodom, I will spare the whole place for their sake."

Then Abraham spoke up again: "Now that I have been so bold as to speak to the Lord, though I am nothing but dust and ashes, what if the number of the righteous is five less than fifty? Will you destroy the whole city because of five people?"

"If I find forty-five there," he said, "I will not destroy it."

Once again he spoke to him, "What if only forty are found there?"

He said, "For the sake of forty, I will not do it."

Then he said, "May the Lord not be angry, but let me speak. What if only thirty can be found there?"

He answered, "I will not do it if I find thirty there."

Abraham said, "Now that I have been so bold as to speak to the Lord, what if only twenty can be found there?"

He said, "For the sake of twenty, I will not destroy it."

Then he said, "May the Lord not be angry, but let me speak just once more. What if only ten can be found there?"

He answered, "For the sake of ten, I will not
destroy it."
When the LORD had finished speaking with
Abraham, he left, and Abraham returned home.
(Genesis 18:20–33)

Theologians from many different backgrounds find common ground in the important role of prayer. John Wesley is
frequently quoted as having said, "God will do nothing in the
affairs of men except in answer to believing prayer." John
Calvin affirmed that the providence of God does not exclude
the exercise of human faith. While God neither sleeps nor
slumbers, Calvin said, "He is inactive, as if forgetting us, when
He sees us idle and mute."[4] Jack Hayford says, "You and I can
help decide which of these two things—blessing or cursing—
happens on earth. We will determine whether God's goodness
is released toward specific situations or whether the power of
sin and Satan is permitted to prevail. Prayer is the determining
factor."[5] As Walter Wink is fond of saying, "History belongs to
the intercessors."[6]

The Bible often uses language that ascribes human form or
attributes to God, and as a result, it appears that God changes his
mind in light of new input. If this were true in an absolute sense,
it would mean that at least some of God's decisions were initially
inadequate or ill-informed and in need of revision. Based on
God's perfect character, we know that isn't true. So it appears
that these passages provide us with a relative—rather than an
absolute—perspective to stress the dignity of human choice and
interaction with God.

MEN OF ISSACHAR

Every human being has made at least one poor decision.
Most of us have a catalog of bad choices, and we revisit
them from time to time, imagining how things might have

turned out if we had chosen wisely. Dante Gabriel Rossetti, a nineteenth-century English painter and poet whose works were focused almost exclusively on his beautiful wife Elizabeth, was overwhelmed with grief when she took her own life just two years after their wedding. Rossetti took his poems, put them in her coffin, and buried them with her. Years later, after his grieving process was over, Rossetti wondered if some of his greatest poetry should remain underground. With great effort, he finally persuaded the authorities to exhume the coffin and retrieve the poems. In 1870, they were published to great acclaim, as his greatest works.

Unlike Rossetti, however, we rarely have the chance to undo foolish choices. We make decisions every day, and the patterns established by the small decisions shape the course of the larger ones.

From 1 Chronicles 12:32, we find two key prerequisites for good decision making: "Men of Issachar ... understood the times and knew what Israel should do." This little nugget is tucked away in the middle of a listing of the men who had volunteered to serve David and who supported his anointing as king over all Israel. The description of these unique men underscores two essential components of effective decision making: awareness and decisiveness. Good decisions require adequate information and careful analysis of all of the pertinent facts. Although there is a place for spontaneity, important decisions generally should not be rushed, since they require sufficient time for gestation. But, once made, such decisions should be decisively communicated and implemented. Like the men of Issachar, as leaders we need to understand the times and be well aware of the cultural climate in which we live and work, so that we may become transformers rather than conformers.

In 1982 Pope John Paul II established the Pontifical Council for Culture because of his conviction that "the destiny of the world" hinges on "the Church's dialogue with the cultures of our time." Admitting that theology must be contextualized,

Pope John Paul insisted that "the synthesis between culture and faith is not just a demand of culture, but also of faith. A faith which does not become culture is a faith which has not been fully received, not thoroughly thought through, not fully lived out."[7] We are not to be bound by our culture; we are to transcend it and transform it.

The old adage is true: There are two sides to every issue, but there are also two sides to a sheet of flypaper, and it makes a big difference to the fly which side he chooses. At the end of the day, we all have to make choices, and once those choices are made, we have to live with them. That was Hamlet's difficulty—determining a course of action—as evidenced through his lines from the famous "To be or not to be" speech:

> And thus the native hue of resolution
> Is sicklied o'er with the pale cast of thought,
> And enterprises of great pith and moment
> With this regard their currents turn awry,
> And lose the name of action
>
> —*Hamlet*, act 3, scene 1

What the young Prince of Denmark was saying is that he waffled back and forth. He fluctuated between two options and could not decide on a course of action. By not making a choice, he, in fact, chose badly. In any area, this is true: No decision is a decision to remain in the status quo, to shirk an opportunity for growth, to make ourselves and our image of God a little bit smaller.

Deciding Wisely

Good decisions require accurately processed information. Technology has made it relatively easy to gather information. Computers crunch data and give it out in digestible bits, but the human mind must still analyze that data and make decisions based on it. Because Solomon knew that leaders must make good decisions, he urged them to attain wisdom and mental discipline and to understand words of insight:

> The proverbs of Solomon son of David, king of Israel:
> for attaining wisdom and discipline; for understand-
> ing words of insight; for acquiring a disciplined and
> prudent life, doing what is right and just and fair; for
> giving prudence to the simple, knowledge and discre-
> tion to the young—let the wise listen and add to
> their learning, and let the discerning get guidance—
> for understanding proverbs and parables, the sayings
> and riddles of the wise. (Proverbs 1:1–6)

In an age in which computer technology helps us to gather and analyze incredible amounts of data, the pithy bits of wisdom found in the ancient book of Proverbs are more important than ever. As decision makers, we must understand complicated matters, but we also need God's perspective in deciding how to act. The book of Proverbs helps us do just that.

As leaders, we must develop disciplined and prudent characters so that we will do what is right and just and fair. The rub comes when we don't know what is just and right and fair—or when any conceivable decision appears unjust, wrong, and unfair. That is why Solomon cautioned that the unsophisticated need prudence. The young need knowledge and discretion. In fact, everyone needs to foster learning and seek guidance on a daily basis.

Proverbs isn't a decision-making textbook, but this wisdom-packed book is God's gift to help us make the best decisions possible. The introductory verses tell us that the proverbs that follow will help us develop the mental sharpness needed to process complex information. Even though technology helps us to gather and manipulate information, we must still have sharp minds and apply solid logic and keen insight to that information in order to make good decisions. On this subject Bill Hybels writes:

Human judgment is always limited and sometimes
wrong. Sometimes our best notions about what
ought to be said or done are ill-advised, dangerous,
even destructive. When it comes to the key decisions
in our lives, we almost always need deeper insights
and a broader perspective than mere human wisdom
can offer us.

What we desperately need is God's mind on the
serious matters of life. He offers it to us through the
teaching of his Word and the inner guidance of his
Spirit. Our job is not to question it or to assume that
we know better ... but to trust that God does know
better how to make our lives work. A helpful spiritual rule of thumb might be "When in doubt, always,
always, always trust the wisdom of God."[8]

The proverbs help us to accomplish this goal in a godly manner. They sharpen our minds and reveal God's insight to ensure
that our decisions are in sync with his eternal perspective.

The Danger of Excluding God

No decision is wise if it's made independently of God. In Joshua
9, the people of Israel made a terrible decision because they left
God out of their plans; as a result, they had to live with the consequences of a decision that God did not approve:

Now when all the kings west of the Jordan heard
about these things—those in the hill country, in the
western foothills, and along the entire coast of the
Great Sea as far as Lebanon ... they came together to
make war against Joshua and Israel.

However, when the people of Gibeon heard what
Joshua had done to Jericho and Ai, they resorted to a
ruse: They went as a delegation whose donkeys were
loaded with worn-out sacks and old wineskins,
cracked and mended. The men put worn and patched
sandals on their feet and wore old clothes. All the

bread of their food supply was dry and moldy. Then they went to Joshua in the camp at Gilgal and said to him and the men of Israel, "We have come from a distant country; make a treaty with us."

The men of Israel said to the Hivites, "But perhaps you live near us. How then can we make a treaty with you?"

"We are your servants," they said to Joshua.

But Joshua asked, "Who are you and where do you come from?"

They answered: "Your servants have come from a very distant country because of the fame of the LORD your God. For we have heard reports of him: all that he did in Egypt, and all that he did to the two kings of the Amorites east of the Jordan.... And our elders and all those living in our country said to us, 'Take provisions for your journey; go and meet them and say to them, "We are your servants; make a treaty with us."' This bread of ours was warm when we packed it at home on the day we left to come to you. But now see how dry and moldy it is. And these wineskins that we filled were new, but see how cracked they are. And our clothes and sandals are worn out by the very long journey."

The men of Israel sampled their provisions *but did not inquire of the LORD*. Then Joshua made a treaty of peace with them to let them live, and the leaders of the assembly ratified it by oath. (Joshua 9:1–15)

The Israelites gathered data (vv. 7–14), but they missed a crucial step in the process. "The men of Israel ... did not inquire of the LORD" (v. 14). Many years later, James addressed this very same issue when he wrote, "You ought to say, 'If it is the Lord's will, we will live and do this or that'" (James 4:15).

In *Decision Making by the Book*, Haddon Robinson comments on James' statement: "James is not against making plans ... he is not taking a cheap shot at charts or making an argument against commitments.... What James warns us about is that our freedom to make plans is not a license to live free from God. To come to that conclusion would be arrogant." In fact, Robinson asserts, "The phrase, 'If it is the Lord's will,' ought to infect our thinking. It ought to be a standard part of our vocabulary."[9]

In this instance, Joshua failed to consult God and therefore made a bad decision. In the end he was obligated to hold himself and his people to his commitment to the Gibeonites—a commitment that prevented Israel from fully conquering Canaan. While Joshua did, finally, make the best of a bad situation, the end results were far from optimal. James urged anyone who believes in the sovereign God to consult him before making decisions. Robinson reminds us again: "You and I are never free from God. We must make our decisions in submission to His sovereign will."[10]

Ronald Reagan once declared: "America was founded by people who believed that God was their rock of safety. He is ours. I recognize we must be cautious in claiming that God is on our side, but I think it's all right to keep asking if we're on His side."[11] If we blithely assume that God is always on our side, we will fall headlong into foolishness. We should search ourselves regularly to make sure our thinking is in line with his will. We should strive to develop the character and conviction to make decisions that are products of our relationship with God.

THE DECISION-MAKING PROCESS

Decision making is one of leadership's core competencies. In fact, decision-making ability differentiates between poor and good, and between good and great, leaders. Decisions reveal values and intelligence. They require obedience to and dependence upon God. They demand wisdom. Making decisions affects just about everything else leaders do.

Let's examine a leader who depended upon God and consequently had a proven track record in decision making. Of all the

Bible's leaders, Nehemiah provides one of the best patterns for making wise decisions in the right way:

> In the month of Kislev in the twentieth year, while I was in the citadel of Susa, Hanani, one of my brothers, came from Judah with some other men, and I questioned them about the Jewish remnant that survived the exile, and also about Jerusalem.
>
> They said to me, "Those who survived the exile and are back in the province are in great trouble and disgrace. The wall of Jerusalem is broken down, and its gates have been burned with fire."
>
> When I heard these things, I sat down and wept. For some days I mourned and fasted and prayed before the God of heaven. Then I said:
>
>> O LORD, God of heaven, the great and awesome God, who keeps his covenant of love with those who love him and obey his commands, let your ear be attentive and your eyes open to hear the prayer your servant is praying before you day and night for your servants, the people of Israel. I confess the sins we Israelites, including myself and my father's house, have committed against you. We have acted very wickedly toward you. We have not obeyed the commands, decrees and laws you gave your servant Moses.
>>
>> Remember the instruction you gave your servant Moses, saying, "If you are unfaithful, I will scatter you among the nations, but if you return to me and obey my commands, then even if your exiled people are at the farthest horizon, I will gather them from there and bring them to the place I have chosen as a dwelling for my Name."

> They are your servants and your
> people, whom you redeemed by your great
> strength and your mighty hand. O Lord, let
> your ear be attentive to the prayer of this
> your servant and to the prayer of your ser-
> vants who delight in revering your name.
> Give your servant success today by grant-
> ing him favor in the presence of this man.
>
> I was cupbearer to the king. (Nehemiah 1:1–11)

Nehemiah was faced with a huge challenge. The walls of Jerusalem were in disrepair, and the returned exiles were vulnerable and disheartened. When Nehemiah received this news in exile, he began a four-step process to approach the problem. First, he carefully studied the situation (vv. 2–3). Second, he empathized with those who were hurting (v. 4). Third, he humbled himself before God (v. 4). Fourth, he prayed (vv. 5–11). And what a prayer! Nehemiah adored God (v. 5), confessed his nation's sin to the Lord (vv. 6–7), and finally petitioned God for help (vv. 8–11).

Ultimately, Nehemiah knew what every great leader knows: All wisdom comes from God, and he wants to help us learn to use his wisdom to make good decisions. Prayer, then, must become a permanent part of our decision-making process, even in the arena of business. The fact that it may strike us as an odd notion to pray over business decisions reveals how we have fallen prey to the false notion that there is a distinction between the sacred and the secular. As fully developing followers of Jesus, however, our calling is to do *everything* in the name of the Lord (Colossians 3:17)—which includes making decisions.

1. Lewis Carroll, *Alice's Adventures in Wonderland* (New York: Alfred A. Knopf, 1984), 89.
2. Philip Yancey, *The Bible Jesus Read* (Grand Rapids, MI: Zondervan, 1999), 33.

3. Abraham J. Heschel, "The Divine Pathos," in *Judaism*, vol. 11, no. 1 (January 1963), 61.

4. See John Calvin, *Institutes of the Christian Religion*, Book III:XX:2–3.

5. Jack W. Hayford, *Prayer Is Invading the Impossible* (New York: Ballantine Books, 1983), 57.

6. The first time this phrase appeared was in Wink's article "Prayer and the Powers" in *Sojourners* (October 1990), 10.

7. Pope John Paul II, letter to Agostino Cardinal Casaroli, secretary of state, May 20, 1982, as quoted in *Inculturation: Its Meaning and Urgency*, by J. M. Waliggo, A. Roest Crollius, T. Nkeramihigo, and J. Mutiso-Mbinda (Kampala, Uganda: St. Paul Publications, 1986), 7. Quoted from letter to Agostino Cardinal Casaroli on the occasion of the creation of the Pontifical Council for Culture, *Osservatore Romano* (English edition), June 28, 1982, 7.

8. Bill Hybels, *Making Life Work* (Downers Grove, IL: InterVarsity Press, 1998), 203.

9. Haddon Robinson, *Decision Making by the Book* (Grand Rapids, MI: Chariot Victor Publishing, 1991), 64–66.

10. Ibid.

11. This quotation was taken from his 1984 State of the Union address. Reagan clearly was alluding to Lincoln's famed reply to the question of whose side God was on: "My great concern is not whether God is on our side; my great concern is to be on God's side."

CHAPTER 10

Problem Solving

FOCUS ON THE SOLUTION, NOT THE PROBLEM

God is the utmost problem solver, and he provides resources for his people to solve the problems they encounter. The problem is that we are generally disinclined to lay hold of them. We typically attempt to solve our own problems without appealing for divine provision, calling on God only when we are in real trouble. For some reason it doesn't occur to us that the God of the Bible knows much about business or investments or staffing issues. We go to God with our emotional problems or our family disputes, but we doubt his competence in other areas. Sometimes we act as if we aren't even convinced that God is concerned with such mundane areas of our lives as mortgage payments and vacation plans. We seem to be unaware that there is untapped wisdom to be found in taking *everything* to him.

We have a tendency to think that God is concerned only with the midsized problems in our lives. We may think there are some problems that are too trivial for him to be interested in. On the other hand, we also assume that there are some problems that are too big to take to him. There is a great biblical example of two people who responded to a problem that seemed insurmountable; it is found in Esther 3:1—5:8.

The book of Esther recounts a fascinating story filled with

intrigue and suspense. Esther was a Jewish orphan who had been raised by her older cousin Mordecai (2:7). When she was old enough, the Persian King Xerxes selected Esther as his queen (2:17). Because of his convictions, Mordecai refused to kneel down in deference to Haman, a sinister official in Xerxes' court (3:2–5). In anger, Haman devised a cunning plot that resulted in a decree to execute all of the Jews in the Persian Empire (3:6–15).

It appeared that all would be lost. The Messianic line was in danger of extinction, and God's people were powerless to defend themselves. Mordecai was at first overwhelmed by the magnitude of the situation, but he soon began to focus his attention on the solution rather than on the problem.

Although the name of God is not directly mentioned in this book, it is evident that Mordecai concluded that God had sovereignly elevated Esther to a position of royalty so that she would be in a position to counteract the deadly edict. She held the fate of history in her hands. But to act could cost her very life (4:9–11). She was the queen of the most powerful empire on earth and enjoyed all of the privileges that such a position afforded her. Why should she risk her life to persuade the king to change a decree, even if it did threaten to destroy her own people?

Mordecai's answer to Esther's fears was clear and concise:

> Do not think that because you are in the king's
> house you alone of all the Jews will escape. For if
> you remain silent at this time, relief and deliverance
> for the Jews will arise from another place, but you
> and your father's family will perish. And who knows
> but that you have come to royal position for such a
> time as this? (Esther 4:13–14)

Esther's solution was marked by radical dependence upon God (4:16), as well as careful thought and creativity. Realizing that an appeal to the king of such magnitude required precise timing, she carefully planned the most appropriate approach for making her request (7:3–6). Later, after Esther had been instrumental in bringing about Haman's downfall (7:6–10), she requested that King Xerxes allow her and Mordecai to write a decree that would overrule the effect of the previous edict and permit the Jews to defend themselves throughout the provinces of the empire (8:1–17).

Esther and Mordecai demonstrate for us how much energy should be invested in dwelling on a problem as opposed to planning the solution. They also remind us that creativity and timing are essential in successful problem solving.

SOLVING THE WORLD'S BIGGEST PROBLEM

The greatest example of problem solving in action can be found right in the pages of the Bible. God took the ultimate problem—the chaos and destruction wrought by human sin—and transformed it into the beauty of holiness through his creative power to solve even the worst of problems. In this best of all stories, God made it possible for those who were previously his enemies to become his beloved children.

Immediately following his introduction to his epistle to the Romans, Paul launched into a description of the greatest problem in human history—God's judgment on humanity as a consequence of man's *un*righteousness and *self*-righteousness. The human solution to the problem of guilt and estrangement from God has always been a tedious series of variations on the same theme—human effort and works. Man-made religious systems always reduce God to a human level or assume that people can bridge the gap themselves. However, because "Jews and Gentiles alike are all under sin" (Romans 3:9), the problem is of such vast proportions that only God can solve it.

The real problem is internal, not external. Jesus said that all the sinful behaviors and habits are inextricably connected to the heart. We can clean up our act, but we need outside assistance to root out the evil in our heart. Any attempt at total self-improvement is like trying to hold ourselves in midair by pulling on our shoestrings.

God's solution is so creative and innovative that no one else could have thought of it or imagined it. It has been common in religious institutions that humans would sacrifice something to the gods or to God, but the idea that God himself would take the initiative and come looking for lost people is unique to Christianity. That *God himself would offer the sacrifice for humanity* is unheard of in any religion other than biblical Christianity. "For what the law was powerless to do in that it was weakened by the sinful nature, God did by sending his own Son in the likeness of sinful man to be a sin offering" (Romans 8:3). By declaring us righteous by his unmerited favor through the price that Christ paid on our behalf, God overcame the estrangement caused by sin and transformed us from condemned criminals into co-heirs with Christ (Romans 8:17).

In the movie *The Last Emperor*, the young boy anointed as leader of China lives a life of luxury with thousands of eunuch servants at his beck and call. "What happens when you do wrong?" his brother asks. "When I do wrong, someone else is punished," the young emperor answers. To demonstrate this fact, he breaks a bowl, and one of the servants is beaten.

In Christianity, God reverses this situation. In the movie, the emperor does wrong, and a servant is beaten; in Christianity, the servants do wrong, and the Emperor is beaten! The grace of God and his gracious offer of salvation in Christ constitute without a doubt the most creative approach to problem solving ever imagined. It took a God of unbounded imagination to come up with it. We can never comprehend the cost of his innovative plan; we can only scratch the surface of God's grace, and his graceful approach to problem solving.

For godly leaders, life and leadership are transformed in the face of this awesome and amazing reality. There has been no greater problem, and no greater problem solver, in the history of humankind. If there are pressing problems needing our action—

whether in our business, in our family, or in our personal life—
we should know that God is waiting to help us.

SOLVING THE RIGHT PROBLEM

E xodus 32:1–35 delivers a wealth of information about problem solving and deserves careful study. Here we discover
the two most important summary principles for problem solving
from a great leader who solved great problems: Moses himself.

> When the people saw that Moses was so long in
> coming down from the mountain, they gathered
> around Aaron and said, "Come, make us gods who
> will go before us. As for this fellow Moses who
> brought us up out of Egypt, we don't know what has
> happened to him."
> Aaron answered them, "Take off the gold ear-
> rings that your wives, your sons and your daughters
> are wearing, and bring them to me." So all the
> people took off their earrings and brought them to
> Aaron. He took what they handed him and made it
> into an idol cast in the shape of a calf, fashioning it
> with a tool. Then they said, "These are your gods, O
> Israel, who brought you up out of Egypt." (Exodus
> 32:1–4)

Aaron faced a serious problem, but he failed to resolve it.
When he realized that his "solution" was creating a bigger problem, he acted again: "When Aaron saw this, he built an altar in
front of the calf and announced, 'Tomorrow there will be a fes-
tival to the LORD'" (v. 5). But this time his action only caused the
situation to career out of control:

> When Moses approached the camp and saw the calf
> and the dancing, his anger burned....
> Moses saw that the people were running wild

and that Aaron had let them get out of control and
so become a laughingstock to their enemies. (Exodus
32:19, 25)

Moses inherited the problem after it had escalated into a cri-
sis, but he did solve it (vv. 20–35). This brief study in contrast
reveals some important principles about how a godly leader
approaches problems. Aaron attempted to solve the wrong problem; Moses addressed the right one. Aaron attacked the
functional problem; Moses confronted the character problem.
Aaron focused on activity; Moses focused on the morality that
was driving the activity (vv. 21, 30).

The details of this chapter yield a wealth of information
about problem solving and deserve careful study. Stepping back
from the situation, we see two summary principles. First, lasting
solutions come from addressing "why" questions—character
questions—instead of "how" questions. Second, great leaders
achieve greatness because they solve great problems. Lesser
leaders limit their energies to addressing lesser problems.

Volumes have been written on problem-solving techniques.
The Bible isn't one of those volumes. What it does do, however,
is demonstrate to us that the most damaging problems are not
solved by correcting behavior. The problems that most need to be
resolved can only be solved by a change of character, a change of
morality, a change of heart. The wisest leaders will help their followers apply God's grace and power to solve the fundamental
human problem of sin. Observe Moses in verses 30–32:

The next day Moses said to the people, "You have
committed a great sin. But now I will go up to the
LORD; perhaps I can make atonement for your sin."

So Moses went back to the LORD and said, "Oh,
what a great sin these people have committed! They
have made themselves gods of gold. But now, please
forgive their sin—but if not, then blot me out of the
book you have written."

See how one of history's greatest leaders defined and solved problems. In all of our reading about problem solving, we must begin where Moses did.

Getting Our Hands Dirty

As leaders, we must face and solve problems. Daniel provides us with a stunning example of problem-solving ability in Daniel 5. King Belshazzar had given a banquet for thousands of people. During the course of their drunken festivities, the king desecrated the gold and silver goblets that his father had taken from the Hebrew temple in Jerusalem.

> Suddenly the fingers of a human hand appeared and wrote on the plaster of the wall, near the lampstand in the royal palace. The king watched the hand as it wrote. His face turned pale and he was so frightened that his knees knocked together and his legs gave way.
>
> The king called out for the enchanters, astrologers and diviners to be brought....
>
> Then all the king's wise men came in, but they could not read the writing or tell the king what it meant. So King Belshazzar became even more terrified and his face grew more pale. His nobles were baffled.
>
> The queen, hearing the voices of the king and his nobles, came into the banquet hall. "O king, live forever!" she said. "Don't be alarmed! Don't look so pale! There is a man in your kingdom who has the spirit of the holy gods in him. In the time of your father he was found to have insight and intelligence and wisdom like that of the gods. King Nebuchadnezzar your father ... appointed him chief of the magicians, enchanters, astrologers and diviners. This man Daniel, whom the king called Belteshazzar, was found to have a keen mind and knowledge and understanding,

and also the ability to interpret dreams, explain rid-
dles and *solve difficult problems*. Call for Daniel, and he
will tell you what the writing means." (Daniel 5:5–12)

Daniel was promoted to an enviable leadership position. He
influenced Babylonian and Persian kings who ruled over great
empires. Belshazzar promoted Daniel because he could "solve
difficult problems" (vv. 12, 16). One criterion that determines
the greatness of a leader is the degree of difficulty of the problems that the individual is willing and able to tackle and solve.

Donald Schon opened his book *Educating the Reflective
Practitioner* in this way:

> In the varied topography of professional practice,
> there is high, hard ground; manageable problems
> lend themselves to solution through the application
> of research-based theory and technique. In the
> swampy lowland, messy, confusing problems defy
> technical solution. The irony of this situation is that
> the problems of the high ground tend to be relatively
> unimportant to individuals or society at large, how-
> ever great their technical interest may be, while in
> the swamp lie the problems of greatest human con-
> cern. The practitioner must choose. Shall he remain
> on the high ground where he can solve relatively
> unimportant problems according to the prevailing
> standards of rigor, or shall he descend to the swamp
> of important problems and nonrigorous inquiry?[1]

Never is this distinction more significant than in the leadership practitioner's role. Great leadership is willing and able to
roll up its sleeves, get down in the dirt, and tackle life's toughest
issues. Daniel did that. And Daniel ranks among history's premier leaders.

In his book on biblical leadership, Lynn Anderson discusses
the level of involvement shepherds demonstrated in the first
century:

Shepherds in Bible days were not day laborers who showed up for work in the morning at a stranger's pasture, put in eight hours, and then went back home. Rather, a shepherd lived with the sheep—day and night, year after year. Shepherds helped birth the lambs. They led their sheep to pasture during the day and protected them at night. The sheep knew their shepherd's touch, recognized his voice, and followed no other shepherd. There was a genuine relationship between the shepherd and the sheep. In fact, through long time and frequent touch, the shepherds *smelled* like sheep.[2]

Leaders are shepherds, mentors, and equippers—all of these descriptions demand relationships. A leader's authority does not come from title or position; it comes from character, competence, and a willingness to invest in other people's lives. As Greg Johnson points out, "We aren't the *persons* of God but the *people* of God."[3] Our new life in Christ is to be lived out in the context of community, under the authority of others, with our destinies interconnected to theirs. It is one thing to be able to solve problems for ourselves, but, as we have seen, biblical leaders use their problem-solving ability to assist others and advance God's kingdom purposes.

NEHEMIAH: GOD'S PROBLEM SOLVER

By the time of Nehemiah, the political, social, and spiritual conditions of Jerusalem were in shambles. Sometime around 587 BC, Jerusalem was destroyed, along with Solomon's temple. This was the third Babylonian campaign into Judah, and each time the Babylonian armies took more and more Israelites captive, resettling them in Babylon. Daniel, Shadrach, Meshach, and Abednego were among those taken during the first invasion.

About seventy years after the first invasion, Cyrus, king of Persia (who had since conquered the Babylonians), gave the Jews permission to return to Jerusalem to rebuild the temple. Under the leadership of Zerubbabel, Israel seemed to be on the verge of becoming a blessed nation again. But the people refused to turn away from the same sins for which God had judged their ancestors in the days of Nebuchadnezzar. The temple was not maintained properly. The people weren't offering sacrifices. They had adopted many of the religious practices of the surrounding nations.

It's no wonder that when Nehemiah heard about the state of affairs in his homeland, he was moved so deeply that he wept. His concern about the condition of Jerusalem consumed him. But rather than launching some ill-conceived plan to save the day, Nehemiah waited for God to reveal what his next step should be. He prayed and planned and prepared. When God finally said, "Now, go and rebuild the city of Jerusalem," Nehemiah was ready to demonstrate the leadership ability God had been cultivating in his heart.

Nehemiah's Problem-Solving Ability

One way in which individuals prove their leadership ability is by using their problem-solving skills. Nehemiah certainly demonstrated his capability in that way. When the walls of Jerusalem began to take shape, Nehemiah's enemies tried to sidetrack him from the project with a number of different strategies. First, they tried to lure him out of Jerusalem by repeatedly inviting him to a summit:

> When word came to Sanballat, Tobiah, Geshem the Arab and the rest of our enemies that I had rebuilt the wall and not a gap was left in it—though up to that time I had not set the doors in the gates— Sanballat and Geshem sent me this message: "Come, let us meet together in one of the villages on the plain of Ono."

> But they were scheming to harm me; so I sent
> messengers to them with this reply: "I am carrying
> on a great project and cannot go down. Why should
> the work stop while I leave it and go down to you?"
> Four times they sent me the same message, and each
> time I gave them the same answer. (Nehemiah
> 6:1–4)

The enemies of God's people knew that if they could distract the leader, it would impede the progress of the entire project. Seeking peace with his neighbors would not have been a bad thing for Nehemiah to do, but it wouldn't have been the best thing. It would not have been the "great project" that God had called him to complete. So, Nehemiah rejected their invitations and focused his attention on the job at hand.

Next they accused Nehemiah of leading a revolt against King Artaxerxes—a potentially devastating lie:

> Then, the fifth time, Sanballat sent his aide to me
> with the same message, and in his hand was an
> unsealed letter in which was written:
>
> > It is reported among the nations—and
> > Geshem says it is true—that you and the
> > Jews are plotting to revolt, and therefore
> > you are building the wall. Moreover,
> > according to these reports you are about to
> > become their king and have even
> > appointed prophets to make this proclama-
> > tion about you in Jerusalem: "There is a
> > king in Judah!" Now this report will get
> > back to the king; so come, let us confer
> > together. (Nehemiah 6:5–7)

The custom of the times was to roll up a letter, tie it with a string, and seal it with clay. But this letter was "unsealed." Sanballat intentionally neglected to seal the letter so its contents would be known by everyone who handled it. His purpose, of course, was to spread the rumor that Nehemiah was trying to establish himself as the king of Judah.

This letter wasn't true, but since when are people that interested in the truth when there is a hot rumor to be spread? This rumor put everything in jeopardy. If the people believed it, they would openly oppose Nehemiah's leadership since they had no intention of cutting ties with the Persian government. If word of this alleged revolution got back to the king, Nehemiah would be in even more serious trouble—back in Susa with a rope around his neck.

We might think Nehemiah would be completely justified in going on the defensive. The workers were already looking for an excuse to quit, and kings never have gone easy on those who entertain ideas of treason. Nevertheless, Nehemiah remained focused on the job at hand:

> I sent him this reply: "Nothing like what you are saying is happening; you are just making it up out of your head."
> They were all trying to frighten us, thinking, "Their hands will get too weak for the work, and it will not be completed."
> But I prayed, "Now strengthen my hands."
> (Nehemiah 6:8–9)

Nehemiah didn't allow himself to get caught up in what might happen. Instead of being distracted from his duties by those who were out to defeat and destroy him, he confronted his enemies quickly, prayed to God for strength, and continued his work.

Finally, Nehemiah's enemies tried to intimidate him into violating the law of God by urging him to seek refuge in the temple:

> One day I went to the house of Shemaiah ... who was shut in at his home. He said, "Let us meet in the

house of God, inside the temple, and let us close the temple doors, because men are coming to kill you—by night they are coming to kill you." (Nehemiah 6:10)

Only priests were allowed into the part of the temple that housed the altar. Nehemiah wasn't a priest. To violate God's law in this way would discredit Nehemiah in front of all the people in Israel. Not only would it be a violation of the Law, it would also undermine his authority as a leader. When word got out that the governor was hiding in the temple, the people would lose their confidence in his ability to lead them.

Again, Nehemiah refused to be distracted from his work. He solved the problem by obeying God and seeking his strength:

> But I said, "Should a man like me run away? Or should one like me go into the temple to save his life? I will not go!" I realized that God had not sent him, but that he had prophesied against me because Tobiah and Sanballat had hired him. He had been hired to intimidate me so that I would commit a sin by doing this, and then they would give me a bad name to discredit me.
>
> Remember Tobiah and Sanballat, O my God, because of what they have done; remember also the prophetess Noadiah and the rest of the prophets who have been trying to intimidate me. (Nehemiah 6:11–14)

If Nehemiah had been leading from a selfish posture, he would have had every reason to run and save himself. But Nehemiah knew it was better to serve God than to preserve his own life. Compared to the "great project" to which he had been called, the threat of assassination was trivial. Nehemiah wouldn't leave his great project even to save his own life; he knew there was something at stake that was bigger than his safety.

THE ONLY WAY OUT IS THROUGH

As leaders, we will face problems. They can't be avoided. In fact, Dave Anderson—founder and chairman of the Famous Dave's restaurant chain—suggests that "if you want to get ahead, go to your [people], and say, 'You got problems? Give me some.' Instead of running away from problems like most people, go after them…. That's the way to get ahead, by solving problems."[4]

The existence of problems is nonnegotiable in a fallen world. The only controllable factor in the face of problems is our response. If we follow Nehemiah's model and are careful to (1) maintain our focus, (2) confront any false accusations against us immediately and with integrity, and (3) pray to God for strength and wisdom, we will find, as Nehemiah did, that God is ready, willing, and able to help.

We should think about who the Sanballats, Tobiahs, and Geshems are in our life, and remember that no matter how powerful the opposition may seem, God is an invincible ally. How much more effective to ask for help from the One who sees and knows all than to try to formulate a solution on our own!

1. Donald Schon, *Educating the Reflective Practitioner* (San Francisco: Jossey-Bass, 1987), 3.
2. Lynn Anderson, *They Smell Like Sheep* (West Monroe, LA: Howard Publishing Company, 1997), 126.
3. Greg Johnson, *The World According to God* (Downers Grove, IL: InterVarsity Press, 2002), 189.
4. Quoted in John C. Maxwell, *Failing Forward* (Nashville: Thomas Nelson Publishers, 2000), 202–203.

CHAPTER 11

Team Building

ORCHESTRATING TEAMWORK

Perhaps *brief* would be the best word to describe a good kettledrum solo. Even the best musicians in the world would have a difficult time coaxing variety out of the huge mother of all percussion instruments. A flute or trumpet makes for much more pleasing and melodious sounds. Still, there are few solo instruments that can sustain our interest for very long. We tend to think of instruments like the guitar or the piano because they can play more than one note at a time.

The long-term attraction of a good orchestra is not its solos, but its symphony. Music is most moving when it blends and balances the sounds of many individual instruments. Mix the melodious violin with the thunderous tuba, add the melancholy cello and the warm French horn—and the minutes turn into hours without our even noticing. Such individually diverse instruments come together to make a sound like no other and sweep us along with them into another place.

The same principle that brings success in the concert hall holds true in the kitchen as well. A good chef mixes ingredients like flour, eggs, and butter—things that by themselves are unappealing; but properly blended, they become mouth-watering dishes.

Likewise, a great leader must know how to bring together diverse elements and create a productive group. Few skills are more important in leadership than the ability to build a team. A mark of a great leader is the number and caliber of the people he can persuade to join him in his lineup. The greatest king of Israel, David, had a team comprised of "mighty men":

> These are the names of David's mighty men:
>   Josheb-Basshebeth, a Tahkemonite, was chief of the Three; he raised his spear against eight hundred men, whom he killed in one encounter.
>   Next to him was Eleazar son of Dodai the Ahohite. As one of the three mighty men, he was with David when they taunted the Philistines gathered at Pas Dammim for battle. Then the men of Israel retreated, but he stood his ground and struck down the Philistines till his hand grew tired and froze to the sword. The LORD brought about a great victory that day. The troops returned to Eleazar, but only to strip the dead.
>   Next to him was Shammah son of Agee the Hararite. When the Philistines banded together at a place where there was a field full of lentils, Israel's troops fled from them. But Shammah took his stand in the middle of the field. He defended it and struck the Philistines down, and the LORD brought about a great victory. (2 Samuel 23:8–12)

Because David attempted mighty things, only the mighty could keep up with him. Those who could not keep pace could not join the team.

"You Can't Do It on Your Own"

Don Bennett was on top of the world. He was wealthier than most of us will ever imagine. He owned a ranch, a ski chalet, and an eight-bedroom waterfront home on Seattle's Mercer Island.

And then everything changed. On a beautiful sunny day in August of 1972, Don was boating with his children when he fell overboard, and the propeller of the boat ran over both of his legs. He nearly bled to death but managed to survive. His left leg took 480 stitches to close. His right leg was gone completely above the knee.

To make matters even worse, while he was in the hospital recovering, his business fell to pieces. Don felt that he had lost everything—except his determination. Amazingly, Don taught himself to ski again. Eventually, he would teach other amputees to ski on one leg. He started another business, Video Training Center, which listed such clients as Boeing and Weyerhaeuser. He started kayaking, and it was then that he began to dream of climbing mountains again.

Don had climbed Mt. Rainier in 1970. He decided to do it again, but he knew he couldn't do it alone. In preparation for the attempt, he hopped five miles a day on his crutches. With a team of four others, he made it to within four hundred feet of the top before they were forced off by whiteout conditions and screaming winds. Four months later, he was training again with his team captain. They trained together for another year before returning to the mountain. He climbed for five days, fourteen hours a day, sometimes hopping, sometimes crawling up the incline on one leg, and on July 15, 1982, Don Bennett touched the summit at 14,410 feet. He was the first amputee to climb Mt. Rainier.

When asked about the most important lesson he learned during the entire ordeal, his response was simple: "You can't do it on your own." He described how during one very difficult trek across an ice field his daughter stayed at his side and with each hop told him, "You can do it, Dad. You're the best dad in the world. You can do it, Dad." He told his interviewers that there was no way he would quit hopping to the top with his daughter yelling words of love and encouragement in his ear.[1]

"You can't do it on your own." That makes a lot of sense! Few, if any, truly outstanding accomplishments can be achieved alone. That is a fact that most of us are aware of. But what is not immediately obvious is that not just anyone can help. Don Bennett did not recruit his helpers in a nursing home. He built a team of people who *wanted* to climb a 14,410-foot peak and, perhaps more important, who *could* climb a 14,410-foot peak. One who attempts mighty feats had better be capable of recruiting a mighty team of willing and able participants.

TEAMWORK AND THE TRINITY

Strong teams functioning at their best reflect similarities to the relationship that exists within the divine Trinity. Scripture records the work of the divine Trinity in the creation of the cosmos (cf. Genesis 1:1–2; John 1:1–3; Colossians 1:15–17). Thus, when a team works together in an others-centered manner, it mirrors, albeit dimly, the creativity and mutual regard that is derived from God himself. As Gilbert Bilezikian has written, "Whatever community exists as a result of God's creation, it is only a reflection of an eternal reality that is intrinsic to the being of God."[2]

The three persons of the Godhead are never independent but always work together in concert. We needn't read very far in the Bible to discover this truth. In the very first verse (Genesis 1:1), we are introduced to God as the initiator and designer of all creation. The second verse describes the Spirit of God hovering over the created world. Notice that the Spirit does not construct the created world; he merely hovers over it—suggesting the role of protector or overseer. Finally, in the third verse, we find the Word of God as the executor of God's will—the agent of creation.[3]

This perfect and harmonious interaction, though obvious from the beginning of the Bible, was especially evident in the way God made it possible for people who were formerly alienated from him to be transformed into his beloved children (Ephesians 1:3–14). This passage, which in the original language of the Bible is actually one long run-on sentence, beautifully extols the work of each member of the Trinity in God's scheme of redemption, work that corresponds to what we have just seen in the first three verses of Genesis 1.

Paul first wrote of the work of the Father in accomplishing our salvation:

> Praise be to the God and Father of our Lord Jesus Christ, who has blessed us in the heavenly realms with every spiritual blessing in Christ. For he chose us in him before the creation of the world to be holy and blameless in his sight. In love, he predestined us to be adopted as his sons through Jesus Christ, in accordance with his pleasure and will—to the praise of his glorious grace, which he has freely given us in the One he loves. (Ephesians 1:3–6)

The Father chose us before the creation of the world and sent his Son into the world so that through him we could be adopted into his family. He planned all this out very carefully and initiated it at just the right time. God the Father is the initiator and designer of our salvation.

Second, the apostle focused on the work of the Son:

> In him we have redemption through his blood, the forgiveness of sins, in accordance with the riches of God's grace that he lavished on us with all wisdom and understanding. And he made known to us the mystery of his will according to his good pleasure, which he purposed in Christ, to be put into effect when the times will have reached their fulfillment—to bring all things in heaven and on earth together under one head, even Christ.
>
> In him we were also chosen, having been predestined according to the plan of him who works out everything in conformity with the purpose of his will, in order that we, who were the first to hope in Christ, might be for the praise of his glory. (vv. 7–12)

The Son makes the Father's plan a reality. In his incarnation, he becomes the God-man, the mediator between God and man. His blood sacrifice on our behalf paid the penalty for our sins so that we could enjoy forgiveness and lay hold of God's purpose for our lives. God the Son is the agent of our salvation.

Third, Paul described the work of the Holy Spirit who seals and guarantees our spiritual inheritance:

> And you also were included in Christ when you
> heard the word of truth, the gospel of your salvation.
> Having believed, you were marked in him with a
> seal, the promised Holy Spirit, who is a deposit guar-
> anteeing our inheritance until the redemption of
> those who are God's possession—to the praise of his
> glory. (vv. 13–14)

The Holy Spirit applies the righteousness of Christ to all those who are in Christ. He has anointed us, holding us as a pledge until we see Christ face to face. The Spirit of God is the protector of our salvation.

Thus, the Father initiated salvation, the Son accomplished it, and the Holy Spirit makes it real in our lives. At the end of each of these three sections the phrase "to the praise of his glory" appears. All three persons of the Godhead are to be praised for their work in bringing us to salvation. The Father, Son, and Holy Spirit perform distinct roles, but they work together in perfect harmony and agreement.

There is much talk about how to build unity among diverse people. If we go back to the analogy of an orchestra, we may recall how that orchestra tunes itself before the performance. The oboist plays the concert pitch (an A above middle C [440 Hz]), then the first violinist plays the note, and the other instruments tune to that pitch. What follows can only be described as a bizarre cacophony at first, as we hear them make that strange sound only an orchestra can make. But once it has calmed down, they are all tuned to one another by tuning to the same instrument.

Jesus Christ is our guiding instrument. His incarnation sounded the concert pitch for all of us. As we yield to the transforming power of the Holy Spirit, we find our own instruments coming more and more into the same key as Jesus. As a by-product of this harmony with him, we find that we are all in tune with one another as well.

"DAVID'S MIGHTY MEN"

King David was the leader of one of the most celebrated teams in the entire Old Testament. This group was the all-star team of his battle-hardened warriors, celebrated for their valiant efforts. These men were ready, willing, and able to step into the battle and lay their lives on the line for the man they knew was God's chosen leader.

Several things stand out as we consider how David pulled his team together. First, David spent time with his men in battle. We need to stick with our team through "tough stuff." We tend to be seriously bonded together by shared experiences.

Second, knowing that they were willing to make sacrifices for him, David made sure that they knew he was willing to do the same for them. When three of his mighty men risked their lives to obtain drinking water for him during a battle, David refused to drink it, proving his commitment to share the risk with them (2 Samuel 23:13–17). We have to genuinely commit ourselves to our team.

Third, David celebrated victory with his team members. Time and again David and his mighty men faced seemingly insurmountable odds and saw God deliver them. We have to recognize victories and take time to celebrate them with our team members.

Finally, David honored his friends. These men were well known throughout the land as "David's mighty men," a phrase that served as a banner to set them apart as extraordinary (2 Samuel 23:8–17; cf. 1 Chronicles 11:10–11). They weren't merely known as mighty men; they were *David's* mighty men. We have to develop our team's sense of identity so we can stand firm in the face of mounting pressure.

Synergy, Mentoring, and Team Building

Today the church, the body of Christ on earth, is not an organization but an organism that manifests both unity and diversity. We are each a part of something; there are to be no spiritual loners in God's family. We are people who journey along the way with other people to whom we are called into a covenant of relationship. When we come to God, helpless and battered, with nothing in our hands, and receive his gift of forgiveness and salvation, we are "buying into a package deal." When we do so God says to us, "If you love me, you must love my people as well."

We live in an individualistic culture, but we are called to be people in relationship. As Greg Johnson has noted, we are not called to be the *persons* of God, but the *people* of God.

One phrase that is easily overlooked in all this discussion of relationship is the first part of verse 14 in Mark 3: Jesus set his disciples apart "that they might be with him." Before they were sent out to engage the world in ministry, the disciples were called to a personal experience with Jesus. Wisely, Christ never wants anyone to talk about Christianity as a salesman but as a witness, someone who has experienced firsthand what he is talking about. There is something about a person who has been with Jesus that is distinctive.

It is wise for us to see how we can invest ourselves in other people so that the things we have learned, the things we have come to value, the things we have built our lives around will live on after we are gone. A prudent mind is always building succession. A prudent mind is always mentoring others who will rise to positions of leadership in the future. An old folk parable says that a wise man is willing to plant shade trees even though he knows he will never enjoy the shade. He is planting them for his children and his children's children.

We see a great example of the relationship between synergy, mentoring, and team building in sports. Many of the great coaches of our era once played for and served under the great coaches of yesteryear. In the 2002 World Series, the Anaheim Angels squared off against the San Francisco Giants. Remarkably, both teams were managed by former teammates Mike Scioscia and Dusty Baker. Both men are among the finest managers in professional baseball, and they will tell what a wonderful experience it was to play for the legendary Tommy Lasorda. Byron Scott coached the New Jersey Nets to back-to-back NBA finals. He directly attributes much of his success to playing under the tutelage of Pat Riley. As the coach of the San Francisco Forty-Niners, Bill Walsh revolutionized the game of football with his "West Coast Offense." At least seven of those who were his assistant coaches have now been head coaches in the National Football League.

THE CHOOSING OF THE APOSTLES

From a large pool of disciples who were following him, Jesus designated only twelve men who would become his apostles. This was such a significant decision that the Lord prayed all night to prepare for it: "One of those days Jesus went out to a mountainside to pray, and spent the night praying to God. When morning came, he called his disciples to him and chose twelve of them, whom he also designated apostles" (Luke 6:12–13). In his account of this incident Mark adds that Jesus appointed these twelve apostles "that they might be with him and that he might send them out" (Mark 3:14).

Jesus knew that this was the team that would be with him for the rest of his ministry, and he was prepared to pour himself unreservedly into their lives. He would still teach the crowds, but from this point on, in private sessions he would begin to pour his plans and his character into these twelve men. Even in the midst of his greatest popularity, Jesus realized that the way to turn the world upside down is to invest heavily in a few who will carry on the mission after the leader is gone.

More than two thousand years later, we can attest to the fact that it worked. Eleven of these twelve men became the foundation of the church, built on the cornerstone of Christ (Ephesians 2:19–20). Jesus' actions, the unshakable reality of the resurrection, and the indwelling power of the Holy Spirit turned a diverse group of men who were characterized by confusion, infighting, and self-interest into a genuinely synergistic team with (and this is perhaps the greatest miracle of all time) an authentic fondness for one another.

A Team of Specialists

Teams are comprised of positional specialists. These individuals have usually been recruited on the basis of individual ability and expected contribution. But they aren't a solid team until their individual strengths combine to produce an outcome that no single member alone could have produced. High-performance teams are tough to build. So we look to the Master Teacher for a demonstration of how to recruit and mold a world-class team.

Jesus formed the most important team ever assembled. This team was developed to continue his work on earth (Acts 1:8–9). Luke recorded the continuing story of the apostles in the book of Acts. The church they led exploded out of Jerusalem, around the world, and across more than two thousand years of history. In his gospel Mark recounts a seemingly insignificant event—the calling of Matthew, also known as Levi:

> As [Jesus] walked along, he saw Levi son of
> Alphaeus sitting at the tax collector's booth. "Follow
> me," Jesus told him, and Levi got up and followed
> him.
>
> While Jesus was having dinner at Levi's house,
> many tax collectors and "sinners" were eating with
> him and his disciples, for there were many who

followed him. When the teachers of the law who
were Pharisees saw him eating with the "sinners"
and tax collectors, they asked his disciples: "Why
does he eat with tax collectors and 'sinners'?"
On hearing this, Jesus said to them, "It is not the
healthy who need a doctor, but the sick. I have not
come to call the righteous, but sinners." (Mark
2:14–17)

Levi may seem like an arbitrary choice, but as we saw earlier, Jesus spent all night in prayer before making his choices. In other words, he chose Matthew intentionally. By choosing a tax collector, Jesus demonstrated two important principles of team building.

First, he recruited specific people for specific reasons. Teams are made up of players. Players have positions. They are expected to contribute something they do well—ideally better than anyone else on the team.

Second, Jesus recruited an "odd" player. He began with a group of Galileans—working men, mostly fishermen, all with strong Jewish backgrounds. Then he inexplicably added Matthew, a tax collector and hated publican, to the mix. As far as the apostles go, Matthew was the most unlikely candidate. As a tax collector, he would have been violently opposed by orthodox Judaism. In fact, the Hebrew word for tax collector (*mokhes*) seems to have as its root meaning "oppression" and "injustice." The Jews simply hated this oppressive system of Roman taxation. They hated the high percentage of taxes. They hated the sheer number of taxes: poll, bridge, road, harbor, income, town, grain, wine, fish, fruit, etc. They hated how their money was spent on immoral and idolatrous activities. But most of all, they hated what Roman taxation represented: Roman domination of the people of God.

Consequently, any Jew who worked for the Roman "IRS" was viewed as a traitor of the worst sort. Matthew was therefore ostracized from all forms of Jewish life, especially synagogue services. J. W. Shepard notes: "His money was considered tainted and defiled anyone who accepted it. He could not serve as a witness. The rabbis had no word of help for the publican, because they expected him by external conformity to the law to be justified before God."[4]

Interestingly, as the writer of the first gospel, Matthew teaches us more about Old Testament prophecies and Jewish traditions than any other New Testament writer. Reading his book we would think that he was a Jew's Jew. What are we to make of this situation? Perhaps Matthew longed for his Jewish roots and yet was hard pressed by his job security. Likely he studied the Scriptures in solitude, coming to independent conclusions and an individual hope of the Messiah. We should learn from Matthew that those on the sidelines who look so antagonistic might just become the greatest members of our team.

As Jesus passed by, he looked at Levi. Most people would have tried to ignore the tax man or sneak past him. Jesus was different. He met Levi eyeball to eyeball and called him to immediate discipleship.

Levi responded immediately and radically. Likely Levi was familiar with Jesus. The Sea of Galilee, especially this shore near Capernaum, was Jesus' "headquarters." Undoubtedly Levi had heard Jesus preach. He may even have witnessed Jesus' call to the four fishermen. Certainly he had collected plenty of taxes from them, especially after the great miraculous catch (Luke 5:4–7). Though the text is a bit confusing on this point, Levi probably closed up shop and then settled accounts with the Roman authorities over him before abandoning his position to follow Jesus. To do less would have been irresponsible and even dangerous, thus jeopardizing the ministry of Jesus.

It was one thing for four fishermen (Peter and Andrew, James and John) to leave their private business in the hands of their fathers (Matthew 4:18–22). They always had the option to return. In fact, after the resurrection, the apostles returned to

Galilee and spent their time fishing (John 21:1–14). However, Levi's situation was different. He had no other options. He was a small member of a large corporate structure. There were eager young publicans itching to sit in his lucrative seat. When he left, he knew he was leaving forever.

In addition to Matthew the tax collector, Jesus also recruited Simon the Zealot (Luke 6:15), who was at the opposite end of the political spectrum from Matthew. Jesus taught his team of individuals to understand, appreciate, and *love* each other. Jesus molded his team into a tightly knit unit. But he recruited each of them on the basis of their individual strengths. He recruited people who would contribute to the other members of the team and to the team's overall objectives.

Teams, by their nature, require specialists. Specialists often differ in personality and views. Team members combine their strengths to help one another to grow and to change their world. Such a diversified team may be tougher to lead—but then training lions is more exciting than feeding kittens!

Trusting the Team

Every competent leader knows the importance of building a team. But how is this team building accomplished? Once again, Jesus provides us with an example:

> When Jesus came to the region of Caesarea Philippi, he asked his disciples, "Who do people say the Son of Man is?"
>
> They replied, "Some say John the Baptist; others say Elijah; and still others, Jeremiah or one of the prophets."
>
> "But what about you?" he asked. "Who do you say I am?"
>
> Simon Peter answered, "You are the Christ, the Son of the living God."
>
> Jesus replied, "Blessed are you, Simon son of Jonah, for this was not revealed to you by man,

but by my Father in heaven. And I tell you that
you are Peter, and on this rock I will build my
church, and the gates of Hades will not overcome
it. I will give you the keys of the kingdom of
heaven; whatever you bind on earth will be bound
in heaven, and whatever you loose on earth will be
loosed in heaven." Then he warned his disciples
not to tell anyone that he was the Christ. (Matthew
16:13–20)

There is one factor that may be more important to effective
leadership than leadership qualities or extensive training.
According to John R. Katzenbach and Douglas K. Smith, effective leaders "simply need to believe in their purpose and their
people."[5] Katzenbach and Smith contend that the stronger this
belief, the more it enables leaders to instinctively strike the right
balance between action and patience as they work to build effective teams.

Nobody illustrated this principle more effectively than Jesus.
When Jesus asked Peter, "Who do you say I am?" he wasn't
engaging the fisherman in an intellectual exercise. If Peter was
to lead the church, he would have to have a grasp on the identity of Christ and his purpose. Peter didn't blink an eyelid before
answering. He boldly declared that Jesus was "the Christ, the
Son of the living God." When Peter confessed that Jesus was the
"Christ," he exhibited an understanding of the Lord's purpose.
He was the Anointed One, the Messiah, the Savior. He had come
to save all who would trust in him.

Jesus responded not only by affirming Peter's God-given
insight, but also by expressing his confidence in the disciple's
future role in leading the church. While theologians may
debate about the exact meaning of Jesus' words, one thing is
clear: Jesus entrusted Peter with a key leadership role. And
that step was crucial to the future development of the team of
men and women who were to storm the Roman Empire with
the gospel.

THE POWER OF SYNERGY

A team is capable of accomplishing things that no individual, no matter how multitalented, could ever do alone. Let's take a little quiz: If two horses can pull nine thousand pounds, how many pounds can four horses pull?

Here's a hint: it's not nine thousand pounds. In fact, it's not eighteen thousand pounds. Believe it or not, four horses can pull more than thirty thousand pounds! If that doesn't compute, it is because we don't understand the concept of *synergism*.

Synergy is the energy or force that is generated through the working together of various parts or processes. *Synergism* can be defined as the interaction of elements that, when combined, produce an effect that is greater than the sum of the individual parts. *Synergy* is a joint action that increases the effectiveness of each member of a team. To function well, a team must be committed to a common vision and purpose, and it must be willing to work in unity for the improvement of the whole rather than the advancement of any one member.

1. Adapted from James M. Kouzes and Barry Z. Posner, *The Leadership Challenge: How to Keep Getting Extraordinary Things Done in Organizations* (San Francisco: Jossey-Bass, 1995).

2. Gilbert Bilezikian, *Community 101: Reclaiming the Local Church as Community of Oneness* (Grand Rapids, MI: Zondervan, 1997), 16.

3. Adapted from Bilezikian, *Community 101* (Grand Rapids, MI: Zondervan, 1997), 16–17.

4. J. W. Shepard, *The Christ of the Gospels* (Grand Rapids, MI: Eerdmans, 1939), 143.

5. John R. Katzenbach and Douglas K. Smith, *The Wisdom of Teams: Creating the High-Performance Organization* (Boston: Harvard Business School Press, 1993), 138–39.

Part 3:

THE RELATIONSHIPS OF THE PERFECT LEADER

CHAPTER 12

Communication

UNDERSTAND TO BE UNDERSTOOD

Around the turn of the twentieth century, a wealthy but unsophisticated oil tycoon from Texas made his first trip to Europe on a ship. The first night at dinner, he found himself seated with a stranger, a Frenchman, who dutifully nodded and said, "Bon appetit." Thinking the man was introducing himself, he replied, "Barnhouse."

For several days the ritual was repeated. The Frenchman would nod and say, "Bon appetit." The Texan would smile and reply, "Barnhouse" a little louder and more distinctly than the time before.

One afternoon, Barnhouse mentioned it to another passenger who set the oil baron straight. "You've got it all wrong. He wasn't introducing himself. 'Bon appetit' is the French way of telling you to enjoy your meal."

Needless to say, Barnhouse was terribly embarrassed and determined to make things right. At dinner that evening, the Texan came in, nodded at his new friend, and said, "Bon appetit."

The Frenchman rose and answered, "Barnhouse."

In the famous prayer attributed to St. Francis of Assisi, the petitioner asked God to help him to seek first to understand, over being understood. This principle is the key to effective interpersonal communication. Actually, the book of Proverbs offered identical advice ages before. In Proverbs 18:13 we read, "He who answers before listening—that is his folly and his shame." Earlier in this same chapter Solomon offered a pointed evaluation of anyone who would rather talk than listen: "A fool finds no pleasure in understanding but delights in airing his own opinions" (v. 2).

Learning to Listen

A leader who cannot communicate will not lead well or long. Most leaders spend vast amounts of time and energy developing other skills, such as long-term planning, time management, and public speaking. But what about taking time to develop the skill of *listening*? Those who wish to be good leaders will develop this all-important skill. My friend Arthur Robertson, founder and president of Effective Communication and Development, Inc., wrote his book *The Language of Effective Listening* based on the premise that "effective listening is the number one communication skill requisite to success in your professional and personal life."[1]

Dr. James Lynch, codirector of the Psychophysiological Clinic and Laboratories at the University of Maryland, has documented that an actual healing of the cardiovascular system takes place when people listen. Blood pressure rises when people speak and lowers when they listen. In fact, his studies show that blood pressure is actually lower when people are listening than when they are silently staring at a blank wall.[2] According to Dr. Lynch, listening skills aren't just essential for good leadership; they are essential for good health!

A man goes to the doctor and says, "Doc, my wife's hearing isn't as good as it used to be. What should I do?"

The doctor replies, "Here's a test so you can find out for sure. The next time your wife is standing in the kitchen making dinner, move to about fifteen feet behind her and ask her a question. If she doesn't respond, keep moving closer and asking the question until she hears you."

The man goes home and finds his wife in the kitchen. So, he moves to about fifteen feet behind her and asks, "Honey, what's for dinner?"

There is no response, so he moves closer. "Honey, what's for dinner?"

Still no response, so he steps even closer. "Honey, what's for dinner?"

Nothing. Now he's standing directly behind her. "Honey, what's for dinner?"

"For the fourth time, I said chicken!"

THE GOD WHO SPEAKS

After he wrote the book *The God Who Is There*, Francis Schaeffer wrote several follow-up volumes including *He Is There and He Is Not Silent*, which was written to deal with the most fundamental of all questions: How do we know what we know? Schaeffer's answer to that question is simple: The God who is both infinite and personal not only exists, but he exists as a communicator. The foundational assumption of Scripture is not simply that God exists, but that he has communicated with his people through the prophets and apostles, and most decisively through the personal revelation of his incarnate Son. As a personal and relational being, God is a communicator. William Barry and William Connolly write: "Our faith tells us that God communicates with us whether we know it or not.... He shares himself with us even when we do not know that he is doing so.... We are being 'spoken to' continuously."[3]

Psalm 19 contains a description of two ways in which God communicates with us: *general* revelation and *special* revelation:

> The heavens declare the glory of God; the skies proclaim the work of his hands. Day after day they pour

> forth speech; night after night they display knowl-
> edge. There is no speech or language where their
> voice is not heard. Their voice goes out into all the
> earth, their words to the ends of the world. In the
> heavens he has pitched a tent for the sun, which is
> like a bridegroom coming forth from his pavilion,
> like a champion rejoicing to run his course. It rises
> at one end of the heavens and makes its circuit to
> the other; nothing is hidden from its heat. (Psalm
> 19:1–6)

The first six verses of this wisdom psalm present God's general revelation of himself through the power, order, and beauty of nature. This revelation is general because it is available to all people. Without speech or language, the stars eloquently point beyond themselves to the One who created and sustains them. Therefore no one is really ignorant of God's existence; his "invisible qualities—his eternal power and divine nature—have been clearly seen, being understood from what has been made, so that men are without excuse" (Romans 1:20).

In verses 7 through 11, the psalmist moves from general to special revelation, from nature to the written Word:

> The law of the LORD is perfect, reviving the soul. The
> statutes of the LORD are trustworthy, making wise the
> simple. The precepts of the LORD are right, giving joy
> to the heart. The commands of the LORD are radiant,
> giving light to the eyes. The fear of the LORD is pure,
> enduring forever. The ordinances of the LORD are
> sure and altogether righteous. They are more pre-
> cious than gold, than much pure gold; they are
> sweeter than honey, than honey from the comb. By
> them is your servant warned; in keeping them there
> is great reward.

God's Word richly blesses and empowers those who learn from it and follow it. God communicates with us in Scripture not merely to *inform* us, but also to *transform* us. The New Testament writers are in full agreement with this sentiment:

> All Scripture is God-breathed and is useful for teaching, rebuking, correcting and training in righteousness, so that the man of God may be thoroughly equipped for every good work.
> (2 Timothy 3:16–17)
>
> For the word of God is living and active. Sharper than any double-edged sword, it penetrates even to dividing soul and spirit, joints and marrow; it judges the thoughts and attitudes of the heart. Nothing in all creation is hidden from God's sight. Everything is uncovered and laid bare before the eyes of him to whom we must give account. (Hebrews 4:12–13)

There are benefits attached to consistent exposure to the God-breathed Word. The Holy Spirit will speak to us through the pages of Scripture if we will only come into his presence with open hearts and open Bibles. The Bible isn't merely a book; it is a letter from God to us. In it, he communicates who he is, what he wants for us, how we can respond to his expressed desire, and the best way to order our lives according to our inherent design. The Bible is a map to the abundant life God offers us as his children.

I came to faith in the early part of the summer of 1967, but I had been exposed to the Bible before that night. I had learned Bible verses as a child, but they never meant anything to me. It was like memorizing bits and phrases of Shakespeare or quotes from Mark Twain. They were useful to season a conversation with, but they were far from life-changing. After I became a Christian, however, it started to become clear to me that these Bible verses are qualitatively different from quotations of Shakespeare and Mark Twain. The concepts found in the Bible have the potential to radically alter the course of a person's life. I knew almost immediately that I needed to go somewhere and devote a good portion of my life to learning the Bible. Within six months I went from being a long-haired graduate student in Berkeley, California, to being a well-groomed seminary student in Dallas, Texas. I was willing to cut my hair and wear a coat and tie to class every day (a real culture shock for a former hippie) just so I could learn everything possible about God's blueprint for my life.

But as great as the Bible is, God's highest form of communication is his *personal* revelation through Jesus Christ:

> In the past God spoke to our forefathers through the prophets at many times and in various ways, but in these last days he has spoken to us by his Son, whom he appointed heir of all things, and through whom he made the universe. The Son is the radiance of God's glory and the exact representation of his being, sustaining all things by his powerful word. (Hebrews 1:1–3)

Jesus said that he came to make it possible for us to know the Father: "All things have been committed to me by my Father. No one knows the Son except the Father, and no one knows the Father except the Son and those to whom the Son chooses to reveal him" (Matthew 11:27). Because God has taken the initiative, he has made it possible for us to know him, and he invites us to communicate with him personally through Scripture and through prayer.

THE MOST DISOBEYED COMMANDMENT

It is important to practice such active listening techniques as maintaining eye contact and rephrasing what we hear to be certain that we have understood correctly. George Bernard Shaw believe that the single biggest problem in communication is the illusion that it has been accomplished.

Closely tied in with the skill of listening is the ability to express oneself in a nonabrasive and affirming manner. After all, "Reckless words pierce like a sword, but the tongue of the wise brings healing" (Proverbs 12:18). We may teach our children to say, "Sticks and stones may break my bones, but words will never hurt me," but it is just not true. Words can hurt. Words can cut. In fact, at the root of our word "sarcasm" is the notion of cutting flesh. Anyone who has ever been on the receiving end of sarcastic speech knows the accuracy of that statement.

It may be unhealthy to keep our emotions bottled up, but that doesn't give us the freedom to vent anger, irritation, disappointment, impatience, stress, insecurity, guilt, or whatever negative emotion we may be feeling at the time. Dietrich Bonhoeffer spoke of the need to practice "the ministry of holding one's tongue": "Often we combat our evil thoughts most effectively if we absolutely refuse to allow them to be expressed in words.... It must be a decisive rule of every Christian fellowship that each individual is prohibited from saying much that occurs to him."[4]

Wise leaders think before they speak; in so doing they select words that nurture rather than destroy. When faced with hostility they speak gently, so as to subdue anger rather than stoke it (Proverbs 15:1). In his New Testament epistle, James wrote, "My dear brothers, take note of this: Everyone should be quick to listen, slow to speak and slow to become angry, for man's anger does not bring about the righteous life that God desires" (James 1:19–20). Those three commands (quick to listen, slow to speak, and slow to anger) may be the most frequently disobeyed commands in the whole Bible. If observed regularly, however, they can radically change a person's life and help bring about the righteous life that God desires.

Our degree of ability to communicate will evoke either trust or distrust in those we attempt to lead. It will instill either confidence or fear. It will determine to a large extent how eagerly others will be to hear us, believe us, and follow us.

The Tricky Tongue

Because we have been created in the likeness of God, we are personal, relational, communicating beings. The issue is not *whether* we will communicate, but how effective and appropriate our communication will be. Our speech can be a source of blessing or injury to others as James points out in his epistle. James is the wisdom book of the New Testament, and, like the book of Proverbs, it says a great deal about the words we speak. Chapter three underscores much of what we already know through long and painful experience: The tongue seems to be more difficult to bring under control than any other part of our being.

> We all stumble in many ways. If anyone is never at fault in what he says, he is a perfect man, able to keep his whole body in check.
>
> When we put bits into the mouths of horses to make them obey us, we can turn the whole animal. Or take ships as an example. Although they are so large and are driven by strong winds, they are steered by a very small rudder wherever the pilot wants to go. Likewise the tongue is a small part of the body, but it makes great boasts. Consider what a great forest is set on fire by a small spark. The tongue also is a fire, a world of evil among the parts of the body. It corrupts the whole person, sets the whole course of his life on fire, and is itself set on fire by hell. (James 3:2–6)

Our speech is not neutral territory; it is informed and shaped by our character. The art of listening well and speaking in appropriate ways is rarely taught in the classroom, but these special skills are nevertheless essential to effective leadership.

Notice James' conclusion about our inability to control the tongue: "All kinds of animals, birds, reptiles and creatures of the sea are being tamed and have been tamed by man, but no man can tame the tongue. It is a restless evil, full of deadly poison"

(vv. 7–8). But notice that he doesn't leave us as dangling, help-less victims of our uncontrollable tongues:

> Who is wise and understanding among you? Let him show it by his good life, by deeds done in the humil-ity that comes from wisdom. But if you harbor bitter envy and selfish ambition in your hearts, do not boast about it or deny the truth. Such "wisdom" does not come down from heaven but is earthly, unspiri-tual, of the devil. For where you have envy and selfish ambition, there you find disorder and every evil practice.
>
> But the wisdom that comes from heaven is first of all pure; then peace-loving, considerate, submis-sive, full of mercy and good fruit, impartial and sincere. Peacemakers who sow in peace raise a har-vest of righteousness. (vv. 13–18)

Two sources can animate our speech: wisdom that is earthly or wisdom that is heavenly. Jesus told his followers,

> No good tree bears bad fruit, nor does a bad tree bear good fruit. Each tree is recognized by its own fruit. People do not pick figs from thornbushes, or grapes from briers. The good man brings good things out of the good stored up in his heart, and the evil man brings evil things out of the evil stored up in his heart. For out of the overflow of his heart his mouth speaks. (Luke 6:43–45)

The key to taming the tongue is not the tongue itself, but the heart. The apostle Paul concurred, as he quoted from the psalms:

> As it is written:
>   "There is no one righteous, not even one; there
> is no one who understands, no one who seeks God.
> All have turned away, they have together become

worthless; there is no one who does good, not even one. Their throats are open graves; their tongues practice deceit. The poison of vipers is on their lips. Their mouths are full of cursing and bitterness. Their feet are swift to shed blood; ruin and misery mark their ways, and the way of peace they do not know. There is no fear of God before their eyes." (Romans 3:10–18)

According to Paul, of all the ways we allow our inner wickedness to ventilate, our speech is primary. Our tongue is the initial manifestation of inner depravity and worthlessness. Sinful hearts produce sinful speech.

One of the ways parents can tell if their children are really ill is by the smell of sickness on their breath. Evil speech patterns are the smell of sin sickness in our mouths. We don't just need to have our mouths washed out with soap; we need to have our hearts washed clean with the water of God's Word. We need more than mouthwash; we need to take care of the sickness and inner wickedness that motivates the sin proceeding from our mouths.

The Bible is clear that communication is as much an issue of character as it is a skill. No one can tame the tongue. It will speak out of what fills the heart. Joseph Stowell offers this helpful observation:

> James wrote, "No one can tame the tongue" (3:8). This statement is not intended to cause despair or to justify continued failure, but rather to let us know that self-initiated effort is worthless.... In our desire to transform the tongue from a hellish fire to an instrument of constructive communication, we find ourselves up against a task of supernatural proportions.... Therefore, transforming our tongue requires supernatural strength.[5]

It is not possible for us to tame our own tongues, but it is possible to surrender our tongues to the lordship of Christ. As godly leaders, we should pursue heavenly wisdom and fill our hearts with the love of God so that his wisdom and his love flow from us like an unceasing stream of water.

Beyond Speaking and Hearing to Understanding

Effective communication involves more than just speaking and hearing. Real communication takes place only when both parties move beyond speaking and hearing to understanding. Speaking and listening are means, not ends. People who feel better because they "spoke their mind" or think they have fulfilled their obligation because they "heard him out" inadvertently communicate a message that they don't really want to communicate!

Suppose Jack and Jane, a married couple, have recently been in an argument. If Jack offers an eloquent bit of advice or articulately expresses love to Jane, and Jane doesn't listen or understand, why should Jack feel better? The purpose wasn't for Jack to *say* it; the purpose was for Jane to *understand* it. Yet this routine goes on every day. Or, if Jane courageously explains to Jack why she is angry enough to strangle him, and Jack in turn makes some unrelated comment, then Jack has not heard Jane out. He has not fulfilled his obligation to Jane as a fellow human being, let alone as a husband. In either situation, has this couple established greater mutual understanding? No.

God forewarned Isaiah at his commissioning that he would face similar communication problems throughout his ministry: "[God] said, 'Go and tell this people: "Be ever hearing, but never understanding; be ever seeing, but never perceiving"'" (Isaiah 6:9). The people would hear his message, yet they wouldn't understand it. They might allow his words to pass briefly through their conscious minds, but they wouldn't permit those words to take hold in any meaningful way. God's message through Isaiah would go in one ear and out the other. Otherwise, if the people were to hear and understand the message, "they might see with their eyes, hear with their ears, understand with their hearts, and turn and be healed" (v. 10).

The parables of Jesus were the same way. They were designed to reveal truth to those who would receive it and conceal truth from those who would reject it. If people's hearts are right, they will hear the teachings of Jesus and respond and be healed. But if their hearts are not right, they will hear only a story.

Two-Way Communication

No one would disagree that communication is essential to effective leadership. But we may be surprised by the extent to which open, honest, two-way communication can actually benefit leaders and their organizations. Solomon warns his readers to be on the alert for one-sided communication: "A fool finds no pleasure in understanding but delights in airing his own opinions" (Proverbs 18:2). John Stott tells a wonderful story about Joseph Parker, who served the City Temple in London at the end of the nineteenth century. As Parker climbed into the pulpit one Sunday morning, a woman threw a piece of paper at him. He picked up the paper and read the word "Fool!" written on it. Dr. Parker turned to the people and said, "I have received many anonymous letters in my life. Previously they have been a text without a signature. Today for the first time I have received a signature without a text!"[6]

Communication Requires Interaction

Responsible communication demands interaction. Ted Engstrom observed this kind of one-sided communication in the one place where it shouldn't have happened: a seminar on communication. He writes,

> The seminar leader, well known as the chairman of
> the department of communications at a state univer-
> sity, had failed to communicate. He knew all the

proper language and theories. He projected facts, but not understanding.

Communication is blocked when emotions do not coincide with another's feelings or when there is selective listening on the hearer's part. An appreciation of these factors will enable leaders to take better steps to guarantee effective communication in their own group.

The issue can be put another way. Do you communicate without trying, or do you try without communicating?[7]

Proverbs 18:2 demonstrates that the one-sided communicator comes off looking foolish. But look now at verse 13: "He who answers before listening—that is his folly and his shame." A leader must also hear before answering—that is essential. But in order to be truly effective, that leader must also listen and respond with a mind that is open and searching for a fuller meaning. Then and only then can effective two-way communication begin to take place.

1. Arthur Robertson, *Language of Effective Listening*, Robert B. Nelson, ed. (New York: Scott Foresman Professional Books, 1991), xv.
2. Adapted from James J. Lynch, *Language of the Heart* (New York: Basic Books, 1985), 122–24.
3. William Barry and William Connolly, *The Practice of Spiritual Direction* (San Francisco: HarperCollins, 1993), 33.
4. Dietrich Bonhoeffer, *Life Together* (New York: Harper & Row, 1956), 91–92.
5. Joseph M. Stowell, *The Weight of Your Words* (Chicago: Moody Press, 1998), 16.
6. John R. W. Stott, *The Contemporary Christian* (Downers Grove, IL: InterVarsity Press, 1992), 112.
7. Ted W. Engstrom, *The Making of a Christian Leader* (Grand Rapids, MI: Zondervan, 1976), 153.

CHAPTER 13

Encouragement

THE IMPORTANCE OF HOPE

People cannot live without hope. Throughout history, human beings have endured the loss of many things. People have lost their health, their finances, their reputations, their careers, even their loved ones, and yet have endured. The pages of history books are filled with those who suffered pain, rejection, isolation, persecution, and abuse; there have been people who faced concentration camps with unbroken spirits and unbowed heads, people who have been devastated by Job-like trials and yet found the strength to go on without cursing God and dying (cf. Job 1:1—2:10).

Humans can survive the loss of almost anything—but not without hope.

Hope is what we live on and in. Hope is what gets us from one day to the next. When we are young, we go to school and hope that one day we will graduate. We graduate and hope that one day we will enter into a great career. For many of us, when we were single, we hoped that perhaps one day we would meet the right person and get married. Then, when we got married we hoped that one day we would have children. But even if we do have children, we end up hoping that we will live long enough to see our children go out on their own, be successful, get married, and produce grandchildren for us.

We live by hope, and when hope is gone, endurance and joy and energy and courage just evaporate. Life itself begins to fade. When hope goes, we start to die. One of the most profound proverbs of the Bible says, "Hope deferred makes the heart sick, but a longing fulfilled is a tree of life" (Proverbs 13:12).

It could be argued that the problem is not that we don't have hope—because we do—but that our hope has been misplaced. From the time we are young, we begin looking around and wondering what is going to pay off. Perhaps we will invest our hope in athletics or academics. Perhaps we will invest our hope in beauty and fashion. As we get a little older (but not always wiser) we may put our hope in wealth and status, achievement and prestige.

When we place our hope in the wrong things, one of two things is likely to happen. Either we never make it to the level we had hoped for, in which case we end up envious or bitter. Or we make it to that level only to discover that it doesn't fill our heart. In that case, we end up unfulfilled and disappointed.

With all this in mind, it is easy to see that few functions leaders are called upon to perform are more important than that of keeping hope alive. When others are lost in the dark, trapped in a seemingly endless maze of despair, effective leaders drive away the darkness with positive projections for the future of their organization and each of those involved in it. They know when to come alongside of someone who seems to be in danger of losing hope. They sense when a team member needs a quick admonition or a shoulder on which to cry.

THE GOD OF ENCOURAGEMENT

There are so many attributes of God that it seems mind-boggling to try to contemplate them all. But a major theme throughout the writings of the Old Testament prophets is God as an encourager. He lovingly sought to inspire his people to put their confidence and hope in him. In other words, the message is: God encourages his people because he loves his people. Thus, even when God warned his people of impending judgment, there was always a note of consolation quick at hand. In speaking of coming judgment, his prophets always looked beyond the time of travail to a time of unprecedented blessing. This consolation was a kind of encouragement for God's people to endure discipline and trust that he would be merciful in his justice. Isaiah, for example, began his consolation section with these words: "Comfort, comfort my people, says your God" (Isaiah 40:1). After the people's captivity in Babylon, Jeremiah assured them that it was still God's plan to prosper them and not to harm them, to give them hope and a future (Jeremiah 29:11).

The post-exilic prophet Zechariah is a classic example of a prophet through whom God spoke a tremendous word of encouragement:

> "Come! Come! Flee from the land of the north,"
> declares the LORD, "for I have scattered you to the
> four winds of heaven," declares the LORD.
>   "Come, O Zion! Escape, you who live in the
> Daughter of Babylon!" For this is what the LORD
> Almighty says: "After he has honored me and has
> sent me against the nations that have plundered
> you—for whoever touches you touches the apple of
> his eye—I will surely raise my hand against them so
> that their slaves will plunder them. Then you will
> know that the LORD Almighty has sent me.
>   "Shout and be glad, O Daughter of Zion. For I am
> coming, and I will live among you," declares the
> LORD. "Many nations will be joined with the LORD in
> that day and will become my people. I will live
> among you and you will know that the LORD
> Almighty has sent me to you. The LORD will inherit
> Judah as his portion in the holy land and will again

choose Jerusalem. Be still before the LORD, all
mankind, because he has roused himself from his
holy dwelling." (Zechariah 2:6–13)

The people of Israel had recently experienced the trauma of
the seventy-year Babylonian captivity. After a remnant had
returned to Jerusalem to resettle the land and rebuild their temple, many of them may have wondered if God still had a purpose
for them. They were a small remnant, and the land to which
they had returned was desolate. Jerusalem was in shambles, the
temple had been destroyed—the palaces, the walls, everything
was gone. It may have seemed to them as if God had abandoned
his people in favor of some other group.

It was into this context that the Lord sent his servant
Zechariah with a message of comfort and hope. Zechariah
encouraged the people to complete the rebuilding project by giving them a vision of the Messiah who would one day come to
this temple and bring salvation to his people. Through his
prophet Zechariah, God reassured the remnant that he had
brought them back to the land for a purpose and that his
covenant promises to them would be fulfilled in the Messiah's
glorious reign over the nations of the earth (vv. 11–12). God had
not abandoned his people or his promise! In spite of their history of unfaithfulness, the Lord stated that he would remain
faithful to the promises he had made to them.

Like the children of Israel, the early disciples must have
wondered if God was going to abandon them as Christ told of his
death and eventual return to his Father. After all, they had
invested years of their lives, left behind careers and families in
order to follow this miracle-working rabbi, and now he was
telling them about his impending departure. Jesus comforted his
friends on the night he was betrayed with these words: "Do not
let your hearts be troubled. Trust in God; trust also in me" (John
14:1). Later that same night, he said, "Peace I leave with you;
my peace I give you. I do not give to you as the world gives. Do
not let your hearts be troubled and do not be afraid" (14:27).

God is trustworthy. When our hope is in him, we need never lose courage. Regardless of what happens in our world, his promises are sure. There is nothing that can keep his Word from coming to pass—no adversity, no pain, no sorrow, no setback. Nothing can keep his promise from being fulfilled. Ultimately, we will be with him in his eternal dwelling place. This simple truth gives us comfort and hope in the midst of tough times here on earth.

Andy Cook tells us how we may walk through times of trouble without losing our confidence:

> How will you walk in confidence toward your future? Focus on the blessings, the peace, and the joy that Christ offers. Focus on the fact that Jesus has walked first, inviting us to come with him. We don't have to travel alone. It might be dark, descending into the valley of hell, but at least we're not alone. Jesus promised that he would never, ever leave us. As Paul said in that tiny verse of Philippians [4:5], let your countenance be known to all men, a countenance of confidence that knows, in faith, that "the Lord is near."
>
> Let his attitude be your cloak. Let his sandals guide your footsteps. And as you go, remember that the laughter is just beyond the pain. Just beyond the cross is resurrection. Just beyond the grief is wild celebration. Focus on the laughter that is to come.[1]

God, the Ruler of the universe, cares about encouraging us. He makes it his business to provide his people a sense of comfort and peace—even in the midst of fear and uncertainty. But the way he normally provides his encouragement *for* his people is *through* his people. It is no wonder, then, that our enemy so often uses other people to sabotage and undermine God's purposes for our lives. Joyce Heatherley has written a marvelous little book called *Balcony People*, in which she discusses the pain caused by people who feel the need to constantly evaluate our shortcomings and the joy brought by people who affirm our potential. She writes:

> I am more convinced than ever that if our inner brokenness is ever to be made whole, and if we are to ever sing again, we will need to deal with the issues of evaluators and affirmers in our lives. I also firmly believe that the need for affirming one another is crucial to our process of becoming real, not phony or hypocritical, people of God. Affirming brings authenticity and credibility to our faith as it is lived day by day.[2]

BEING AN ENCOURAGEMENT TO OTHERS

As we become more like Jesus, we must make it our business to provide encouragement to the people around us. In this way, we will find his promise of comfort and peace becoming a greater reality in our own lives.

We need others to walk with us through the peaks and valleys of life. The power of peers walking together in peace and in truth is incredible and necessary for us to be the leaders God has called us to be. We all need to know that there are people who are committed to looking out for our best interests, people who think of ways to stimulate and encourage us toward love and good deeds.

We in turn need to consider ways in which we can encourage others. A phone call, a brief note, or a personal word of thanks for what another person has meant to us requires little time but yields positively disproportionate benefits. We should take the time to thank each person who has made an investment in our life. When the Lord accomplishes something good through us, we should let the person know that another dividend has just been paid on that individual's investment in us.

Encouragement and Human Worth

Encouragement is to a team what wind is to a sail—it moves people forward. Like the ancient Hebrew Christians, we all need words of support. The recipients of the letter to the Hebrews needed encouragement. The fires of persecution were burning so intensely that the believers were tempted to forsake the living God. Because the author knew about this situation, he urged the Hebrew believers to offer daily reassurance to one another: "But encourage one another daily, as long as it is called Today, so that none of you may be hardened by sin's deceitfulness" (Hebrews 3:13).

Of course, encouragement is something each of us as a leader needs to offer our team members. In his capacity as the leader of Outreach of Hope, a ministry geared to instill hope in cancer patients, amputees, and their families, former major-league baseball great Dave Dravecky urges his readers to offer encouragement that validates a person's worth before God.

Dravecky notes: "It's easy for us to confuse our true worth with our sense of worth. While the Bible teaches that our true worth never varies, since it's based on God and not on us, our sense or feeling of worth can vary tremendously."[3] The problem is that feelings don't always align with truth. So what should we do to encourage people who are caught in an adverse situation? First, we need to help them to acknowledge their feelings and to align them with the truth. As people who are made in the image of God, our worth isn't tied into material things that can be bought at a shopping mall, nor is it rooted in a position of power.

Next, Dravecky urges his readers to help those who are struggling with self-worth to find work that is productive and that strengthens their relationship with God and other people. Finding productive work is an important, God-given means to help men and women to sense their intrinsic worth as sons and daughters of God. When we figure out why we are here and what we are supposed to be doing with our lives, God infuses us with a sense of hope and encouragement. We can then pass that same encouragement and hope on to others.

BARNABAS—NO REGULAR JOE

No other New Testament character illustrates the ability to encourage more strongly than Barnabas, whose name means "Son of Encouragement" (Acts 4:36). Think of it: here was a man named Joseph, a Levite from Cyprus. He was a wealthy and generous man who somehow earned a wonderful nickname. What must he have done to impress the apostles to such an extent that they said, "Joseph isn't an accurate name for you; your name should be Barnabas because you are such an encouragement"?

Luke tells us:

> When [Saul] came to Jerusalem, he tried to join the
> disciples, but they were all afraid of him, not believ-
> ing that he really was a disciple. But Barnabas took
> him and brought him to the apostles. He told them
> how Saul on his journey had seen the Lord and that
> the Lord had spoken to him, and how in Damascus
> he had preached fearlessly in the name of Jesus.
> (Acts 9:26–27)

The disciples in Jerusalem were understandably afraid of Saul of Tarsus. Before his conversion, Saul had done everything in his power to destroy the church (vv. 1–2). It is no wonder they questioned the validity of his profession of faith in Christ. As a devout Pharisee, Saul had doggedly hunted down and persecuted followers of Jesus; therefore to the wary disciples, this newfound faith of Saul's could be just another one of his tricks.

Due to their suspicion, it seemed as if Saul's ministry would founder before it ever got started. And that might have happened had not Barnabas been willing to "stand in the gap" (cf. Ezekiel 22:30) beside Saul, leading him to the apostles and testifying concerning his conversion and subsequent ministry. Barnabas encouraged the apostles to bless Saul's ministry, and they responded favorably. Barnabas provided the timely support that Saul needed to launch his ministry.

Perhaps this is one reason why Saul (who was later known as Paul) spoke so often of total forgiveness and the encouraging hope it provides. He had experienced it in a tangible way through the ministry of the "Son of Encouragement." Had Barnabas not offered his hand in fellowship to this penitent man whose life had been turned absolutely upside down, Saul may never have been able to fully experience the freedom he so loudly proclaimed to others. As Jim McGuiggan writes,

> The trouble is, you see, they [the remorseful and penitent] can't enjoy the forgiveness God has freely given them, because you, we, make them doubt it. They haven't the strength or assurance to live in the joy and freedom of a gracious God's free-flowing grace.[4]

Effective leaders, like Barnabas, sustain hope by offering words of support. Suppose for a moment that Barnabas had said nothing on Saul's behalf. What might have happened? In what ways did his actions demonstrate both love and courage? Think for a moment how we can follow his example, whether with a family member, a co-worker, or a peer. A little bit of encouragement can go a long way toward motivating those around us.

The Encouragement of a Friend

In the rough-and-tumble circumstances of life, we sometimes receive blows that leave us bleeding and gasping for breath. During such times, we need reassurance from God and others so that we may remain faithful in "the good fight of the faith"

(1 Timothy 6:12), "fix our eyes on Jesus" (Hebrews 12:2), and "finish the race" (Acts 20:24).

Jonathan and David entered into a deep and profound, covenantal relationship of mutual support that served both men well and gave them steadiness and comfort in unstable times.

> After David had finished talking with Saul, Jonathan became one in spirit with David, and he loved him as himself. From that day Saul kept David with him and did not let him return to his father's house. And Jonathan made a covenant with David because he loved him as himself. Jonathan took off the robe he was wearing and gave it to David, along with his tunic, and even his sword, his bow and his belt.
> (1 Samuel 18:1–4)

These men walked together, prayed for one another, and encouraged one another until Jonathan's death. David would eventually say of his friend, "Jonathan, my brother; you were very dear to me. Your love for me was wonderful, more wonderful than that of women" (2 Samuel 1:26).

Jonathan encouraged David by demonstrating his loyalty to him in the good times, when David was the favorite member of Saul's court. But later, when his father Saul wanted to kill David, Jonathan's encouragement was far more important to his friend. Many people who encouraged David in the good times abandoned him when he most needed support.

In this trying situation, Jonathan modeled the character of the encourager. When David could give nothing in return, Jonathan upheld him by offering his total support:

> Then David fled from Naioth at Ramah and went to Jonathan and asked, "What have I done? What is my crime? How have I wronged your father, that he is trying to take my life?"
>
> "Never!" Jonathan replied. "You are not going to die! Look, my father doesn't do anything, great or

small, without confiding in me. Why would he hide
this from me? It's not so!"

But David took an oath and said, "Your father
knows very well that I have found favor in your
eyes, and he has said to himself, 'Jonathan must not
know this or he will be grieved.' Yet as surely as the
LORD lives and as you live, there is only a step
between me and death."

Jonathan said to David, "Whatever you want me
to do, I'll do for you." (1 Samuel 20:1–4)

Imagine how David must have felt knowing that, despite
great personal risk, his dear friend Jonathan was still standing by
him and doing his best to protect him from harm. Jonathan made
a promise to his friend with no strings attached and proved his
willingness to put himself in harm's way to protect David:

"Why should [David] be put to death? What has he
done?" Jonathan asked his father. But Saul hurled
his spear at him to kill him. Then Jonathan knew
that his father intended to kill David.

Jonathan got up from the table in fierce anger;
on that second day of the month he did not eat,
because he was grieved at his father's shameful treatment of David. (vv. 32–34)

Because of Saul's violent temper, Jonathan and David were
forced to part. The intense drama of their final separation was
played out in an open field. David bowed three times before
Jonathan, face down in the dirt. They kissed each other, each
weeping on the other's shoulder (v. 41).

Jonathan verbally encouraged David in their frequent meetings, and that was important to David. But no words in the world
can match the reassurance of knowing that someone believes in
us and cares enough about us to stand with us no matter how
tough things get or what it costs him. Encouragement in the good
times shows care and thoughtfulness. Encouragement in the

tough times reflects character and commitment. Often, those who encourage during good times abandon us when we need them the most. Jonathan, however, demonstrated godly character by remaining steadfast in the times of hardship.

Encouragement in Times of Trouble

Paul's life in general, and his farewell address to the Ephesian elders in particular, provide us some good insight into the mechanics of encouragement. Paul was a great encourager, not simply because he received such expert encouragement himself from Barnabas, but because he diligently worked at it. After he planted a church, he was conscientious about visiting whenever possible, writing letters and sending others to minister in his absence. He always assured people of his accessibility, even though he may physically have been many miles away or even locked up in a prison cell. Paul's meeting with the Ephesian elders in Acts 20 includes some guidance for the godly leader who wants to uplift others.

First, Paul was able to lend support because his listeners respected his example:

> From Miletus, Paul sent to Ephesus for the elders of
> the church. When they arrived, he said to them:
> "You know how I lived the whole time I was with
> you, from the first day I came into the province of
> Asia. I served the Lord with great humility and with
> tears, although I was severely tested by the plots of
> the Jews. You know that I have not hesitated to
> preach anything that would be helpful to you but
> have taught you publicly and from house to house. I
> have declared to both Jews and Greeks that they
> must turn to God in repentance and have faith in our
> Lord Jesus." (vv. 17–21)

If Paul had been unable to speak these words with a clear conscience, the meeting would have been over. He had made an investment of time and had demonstrated by his example that he was a man of integrity. His example was a source of encouragement for these people of God.

Second, Paul didn't gloss over or distort reality:

> And now, compelled by the Spirit, I am going to Jerusalem, not knowing what will happen to me there. I only know that in every city the Holy Spirit warns me that prison and hardships are facing me....
>
> Now I know that none of you among whom I have gone about preaching the kingdom will ever see me again.... I know that after I leave, savage wolves will come in among you and will not spare the flock. Even from your own number men will arise and distort the truth in order to draw away disciples after them. So be on your guard! (vv. 22–23, 25, 29–31)

Supporting people when all the news is good does not set one apart as a gifted encourager. Neither does soft-pedaling bad news. Psychologists Stephen Arterburn and Jack Felton say that one of the signs of a healthy faith is that it is based in reality:

> Growing Christians strive to see the world and their lives as they really are, not through some stained-glass filter, not through the grid of some externally imposed myth or make-believe worldview. They do not feel compelled to "explain away" hardships or events that mystify them, but are willing to live with some ambiguity, trust God to rule the world in righteousness—even if that means difficulty for them.[5]

No matter how grim reality may look, the leader who trusts God must blend God's sovereign presence with motivation to faithful effort (vv. 32–35). Paul's willingness to face reality was a source of encouragement for these elders.

Third, Paul prayed with the elders before his departure and demonstrated genuine love and care for them:

> When he had said this, he knelt down with all of
> them and prayed. They all wept as they embraced
> and kissed him. What grieved them most was his
> statement that they would never see his face again.
> Then they accompanied him to the ship. (vv. 36–38)

Paul's story in this passage demonstrates that encouragement doesn't always accompany auspicious circumstances. Paul was facing hardship and separation from his friends, and their parting was difficult. But his uplifting words despite the coming trials show us that the gift of encouragement must always be related both to God's sovereign power and to the leader's genuine concern. Paul's reliance on the goodness of God was a source of encouragement to them, as it is to us.

In the latter years of his life, C. S. Lewis carried on a remarkable correspondence with an anonymous woman from America.[6] In his letters, Lewis urged the woman to deal with life in an emotionally honest way, acknowledging grief, fear, and anger openly. He also warned her about the danger of allowing anger and fear to drive her away from God. His letters referred often to suffering and the difficulty of dealing with abrasive people. He also wrote regularly about prayer and its place in the spiritual life. In all the letters, there are three themes that continually surface: honestly dealing with one's emotional state, responding graciously to trials and trying people, and being diligent in one's prayer life.

The letters are fascinating to read, but what is most striking is that Lewis bothered to write them at all. He confessed to being often overwhelmed by his workload, and by this time in his life he could hardly write because of rheumatic pain in his arm. Yet, as Clyde S. Kilby notes, the reason Lewis continued the correspondence was because "Lewis believed that taking time out to advise or encourage another Christian was both a humbling of one's talents before the Lord and also as much the work of the Holy Spirit as producing a book."[7] Being a source of encouragement to a fellow Christian was as meaningful to Lewis as anything else he did. His is an example to all of us about the enormous value of spiritual encouragement, of being present with each other, of giving generously to those who may have little or nothing to give in return.

All of this reminds us that we are not called to walk the road of life alone. God kindly gives us the grace of knowing his encouragement and acceptance. He then provides us with the encouragement and acceptance of others. Finally, he invites us to participate with him in the giving of these same gifts to those who follow our lead.

1. Andy Cook, *A Different Kind of Laughter: Finding Joy and Peace in the Deep End of Life* (Grand Rapids, MI: Kregel Publications, 2002), 77.
2. Joyce Landorf Heatherley, *Balcony People* (Austin, TX: Balcony Publishing, 1984), 25.
3. Dave Dravecky with Connie Neal, *Worth of a Man* (Grand Rapids, MI: Zondervan, 1996).
4. Jim McGuiggan, *The God of the Towel* (West Monroe, LA: Howard Publishing Company, 1997), 100.
5. Stephen Arterburn and Jack Felton, *More Jesus, Less Religion: Moving from Rules to Relationships* (Colorado Springs: WaterBrook Press, 2000), 4.
6. C. S. Lewis, *Letters to an American Lady*, ed. Clyde S. Kilby (Grand Rapids, MI: Eerdmans, 1967).
7. Ibid., 7.

Exhortation

FRIENDSHIP AND LEADERSHIP

Aristotle said, "No one would want to live without friends, even if he possessed every other endowment." Most of us would likely agree with that statement and would gladly tell of important friendships in our lives. But the surprising thing about this quote from Aristotle is its source and its meaning in context.

In his *Nicomachean Ethics,* written in the fourth century before the birth of Jesus, Aristotle (384–322 BC) produced what many philosophers still regard as the most complete book ever written on the subject of ethics and character. He devoted the single greatest portion of that work—nearly 25 percent—to a discussion of friendship. Why would he devote so much of his treatise on human moral behavior to friendship?

Aristotle's answer to this question is anything but obsolete or archaic, and it in fact offers those of us in the beginning of the twenty-first century a refreshing and much-needed perspective on the profound ethical dimensions of true friendship. For Aristotle, the truest friendship is far more than mere companionship, the sharing of mutual hobbies, and a common network of acquaintances. Friends, in the highest sense of the term, are those who make a conscientious effort to take ethics and personal character seriously and inspire each other to be better—in thought, in action, in life.[1]

Leadership is an art. As such, it consists of skills that can be studied, practiced, and mastered. Effective leaders may be found in the boardroom and in the boiler room. They may be teachers, coaches, bankers, lawyers, service station attendants, or food servers. Exhortation is among the relational skills effective leaders cultivate. Exhorters are people who spur others on to higher levels of achievement. In doing so, they help turn their constituents into leaders. But think of the word just used: "spur." Spurring, while it may sometimes be necessary, is not always a pleasant activity.

GOD'S EXHORTATION: "YOU CHOOSE!"

God always cares for his people and desires what is best for them. This is why he taught and exhorted the children of Israel through the many prophets he sent into their midst. Their future, for good or ill, depended upon their responses to God's loving exhortations.

At the end of his life, Moses sought to prepare the generation that had been raised in the wilderness to enter the Promised Land (Deuteronomy 28:1–19). Their well-being depended far more on their spiritual condition than on their military capabilities, and Moses exhorted them to grow in their knowledge of the Lord, to trust him always, and to express this love and trust by obeying his commands.

The blessings for obedience and curses for disobedience that are listed in this passage are not vacuous promises or idle threats. The curses are urgent appeals from a loving heavenly Father who seeks his people's welfare but who will not force them to choose the right path. In this way, God is the perfect model of parenting.

For example, through the prophet Jeremiah, God tells his chosen people, "I know the plans I have for you … plans to prosper you and not to harm you, plans to give you hope and a future" (Jeremiah 29:11). This is surely one of the great promises of God that we would do well to remember. But in the same breath, God says, "You will seek me and find me when you seek me with all your heart" (v. 13).

In other words, God has wonderful plans for his people. His plans are to make us joyful and prosperous, but he will not force his plans on us. We may have his best, we may have joy and prosperity, but only if we choose to seek God with all diligence.

As parents we get frustrated when we see our children choosing something that we know will lead to great pain and harm. Still, we must let our children have certain measures of freedom; otherwise, they will not become fully human. As they get older, as the leash gets longer and longer, the danger is that they may make more and more foolish decisions. But they have to become mature, and we must allow them a certain degree of freedom. Otherwise, we will continue to coddle them and, eventually, rob them of their dignity. Love always contains a risk.

Moses urged the people of God to lay hold of life by trusting and obeying the Lord: "This day I call heaven and earth as witnesses against you that I have set before you life and death, blessings and curses. Now choose life, so that you and your children may live" (Deuteronomy 30:19). There is nothing obscure about that exhortation!

"Those whom I love I rebuke and discipline. So be earnest, and repent" (Revelation 3:19). Because God cares personally about us and our welfare, he warns and urges us to repent and follow his leading while there is still time. He does so through three primary means. First, he uses the convicting ministry of the Holy Spirit. The conviction of the Spirit of God will always be specific rather than general. Satan will tend to accuse in generalities; the Spirit will lovingly lay his finger on specific things that need to be dealt with.

A second means God uses to correct us is the exhortation of

other believers. We should listen for the ministry of exhortation that God provides through others. Most often, this ministry will come from the people who love us the most. Unfortunately, these are often the very ones we tend to take for granted. Still, God can and does use people with whom we are already in covenantal relationships to speak words of encouragement and exhortation to us.

Finally, he also gets our attention with his Word: "All Scripture is God-breathed and is useful for teaching, rebuking, correcting and training in righteousness, so that the man of God may be thoroughly equipped for every good work" (2 Timothy 3:16–17). As we immerse ourselves in the Scriptures, we may frequently find things in the text that call out to us. It may be a word of consolation, but it may also be a word of conviction.

We must remember that revelation always requires a response. God never gives a revelation merely to *inform* us. His desire is to *transform* us, but we must respond to his invitation to be transformed.

Sadly, it is possible to reject the exhortations of God. Repeated over time, this rejection can lead to a seared conscience and an inability to be convicted by the Lord (1 Timothy 4:2). Remember, he tends to speak in "a gentle whisper" (1 Kings 19:12). We can become desensitized to this voice, and God may be forced to use more severe methods in order to gain our attention. He can be incredibly creative in the methods he uses to convict. As C. S. Lewis said, "God whispers to us in our pleasures. He speaks to us in our conscience, and he shouts to us in our pain. Pain is God's megaphone to arouse a deaf world."[2]

At one time or another each of us has sensed God's exhortation through an inner conviction, a portion of Scripture, or a fellow believer. The question is: How did we respond? "My son, do not despise the LORD's discipline and do not resent his rebuke, because the LORD disciplines those he loves, as a father the son he delights in" (Proverbs 3:11–12; cf. Hebrews 12:4–13). Again, there is nothing obscure about that exhortation.

CONFRONTATION: THE GIFT NOBODY WANTS

Some of us are more comfortable with confrontation than others. Sometimes, for various reasons, we prefer to avoid conflict altogether and create what M. Scott Peck calls a *pseudocommunity*—a place devoid of conflict. Here we keep things safe, speak in generalities, and say only things we think others around us will agree with. We are willing to tell small lies in order to preserve the status quo. Pseudocommunity is pleasant, polite, calm, and stagnant—and ultimately lethal.[3]

Regardless of how we feel about confrontation, there are times when confronting is the most loving thing we can do for another person. Dietrich Bonhoeffer wrote: "Nothing can be more cruel than the leniency which abandons others to their sin. Nothing can be more compassionate than the severe reprimand which calls another Christian in one's community back from the path of sin."[4]

Similarly, although being rebuked by another person can be uncomfortable, our openness and willingness to respond to correction, without getting defensive and counterattacking, are critical components of our character.

When John the Baptist exhorted Herod Antipas, saying, "It is not lawful for you to have your brother's wife" (Mark 6:18), Herod responded by having John bound and imprisoned (v. 17). Herodias, the wife in question, cunningly maneuvered her husband into an embarrassing social position in which he was forced to order that the prophet be beheaded (vv. 19–28). Herod's sense of guilt for having done so was evident (vv. 14–16).

Most rulers in the Bible responded unfavorably to prophetic exhortations and rebuke, and this negative response constituted perhaps the greatest occupational hazard of the prophetic calling. Some prophets were imprisoned, starved, tortured, and even murdered as a result of their exhortations. King David's response of repentance to Nathan's rebuke (2 Samuel 12:13) is rare in Scripture, and this kind of conviction is always atypical of people who have been elevated to significant positions of leadership. Nevertheless, it is critical that leaders give and receive exhortations from time to time.

Jesus said, "If your brother sins, rebuke him, and if he repents, forgive him" (Luke 17:3). Paul urged his assistant Timothy to "preach the Word; be prepared in season and out of season; correct, rebuke and encourage—with great patience and careful instruction" (2 Timothy 4:2). Similarly, the apostle instructed Titus to "rebuke [the Cretans] sharply, so that they will be sound in the faith" (Titus 1:13). The necessary balance in exhortation is best achieved by "speaking the truth in love" (Ephesians 4:15). We must give people the gift of truth, but do so in a sensitive and loving manner. As John Ortberg puts it: "There is a very important theological distinction between being a prophet and being a jerk."[5]

In the front of his preaching Bible Warren Wiersbe wrote these words: "Be kind, for everyone you meet is fighting a battle."[6] By writing these words in such a strategic location, he reminded himself that, even as he was preparing to present the truth to people, he had to present it with love, kindness, and sensitivity or the message might not have its desired impact.

"He who listens to a life-giving rebuke will be at home among the wise. He who ignores discipline despises himself, but whoever heeds correction gains understanding" (Proverbs 15:31–32). How do we react when someone exhorts us or rebukes us? "Wounds from a friend can be trusted, but an enemy multiplies kisses" (Proverbs 27:6). Are we sometimes afraid of "wounding" our friends through words of exhortation? If so, we would be wise to heed the advice of Bonhoeffer:

> One who because of sensitivity and vanity rejects the serious words of another Christian cannot speak the truth in humility to others. Such a person is afraid of being rejected and feeling hurt by another's words. Sensitive, irritable people will always become flatterers, and very soon they will come to despise and

slander other Christians in their community…. When another Christian falls into obvious sin, an admonition is imperative, because God's Word demands it. The practice of discipline in the community of faith begins with friends who are close to one another. Words of admonition and reproach must be risked.[7]

Proceeding with Care

When people make inadvertent or careless mistakes, the leader's responsibility to exhort them is tough enough. When people sin and need exhortation, the job is just that much more difficult. Balancing justice and grace, consequences and forgiveness, restitution and restoration, can be confusing. When a leader is angry at and/or disappointed in the offender, the situation becomes even tougher. Because these incidences can become so complicated, God provides help through the words of Paul in Galatians 6:1–5:

> Brothers, if someone is caught in a sin, you who are spiritual should restore him gently. But watch yourself, or you also may be tempted. Carry each other's burdens, and in this way you will fulfill the law of Christ. If anyone thinks he is something when he is nothing, he deceives himself. Each one should test his own actions. Then he can take pride in himself, without comparing himself to somebody else, for each one should carry his own load.

First, Paul defined the purpose of exhortation. It is, simply, to restore. Unfortunately, as Dallas Willard points out, we often confront others in order to "straighten them out." Done in this way, exhortation becomes just another tool of manipulation and coercion.[8]

Once the purpose of exhortation is clear, the process can begin. However, Paul cautioned, the process must proceed "gently," with an attitude of service to the offender. The act must be done in obedience to Christ. The "spiritual one" should act in humility, seeking counsel and accepting responsibility for the manner in which the exhortation is handled.

Because exhortation is important and often so difficult, Paul pointed out that it is fundamentally important who is doing the exhorting. The phrase "you who are spiritual" is *the* most critical guideline in this passage. A. W. Tozer wrote,

> In any group of ten persons at least nine are sure to believe that they are qualified to offer advice to others. And in no other field of human interest are people as ready to offer advice as in the field of religion and morals. Yet it is precisely in this field that the average person is least qualified to speak wisely and is capable of the most harm when he does speak.[9]

Obviously, then, it is vital for those who exhort others to be among those "who are spiritual." But what precisely did Paul mean by this qualification? We should compare and contrast how those guided by the flesh (Galatians 5:19–21) and those guided by the Spirit (5:22–23) would handle the matter of a brother or sister caught in sin. By whom would we rather be "exhorted"? It is no accident that Galatians 6 follows Galatians 5. Tozer continued,

> No man has any right to offer advice who has not first heard God speak. No man has any right to counsel others who is not ready to hear and follow the counsel of the Lord. True moral wisdom must always be an echo of God's voice. The only safe light for our path is the light which is reflected from Christ, the Light of the World.[10]

Before exhorting anyone, the leader needs to engage in self-examination. People fail, and leaders are often compelled to intervene and deal with the consequences. But, Paul reminded

Timothy, gentle restoration handled by spiritual individuals defines the biblical approach to this tough part of leadership.

A Good, Old-Fashioned Rebuke

Sometimes an exhortation may take the form of a chisel and be used to knock off a rough edge. While the process may be painful, it may also be necessary. Indeed, the apostle Paul urged Timothy not only to "correct" and "encourage" but to "rebuke" as well (2 Timothy 4:2). Occasionally a rebuke is the most loving assistance a leader can offer.

In his book *The Management Methods of Jesus*, Bob Briner notes that the word "rebuke" is an archaic term that we don't often hear today. Surely there are occasions in which an old-fashioned rebuke should be the action of choice. But we need to exercise wisdom so that our words build up others rather than tear them down.

Briner notes that not one of the disciples whom Jesus rebuked ever left him. Even Peter, to whom Jesus said, "Get behind me, Satan!" (Matthew 16:23) stuck with him. In fact, the disciples whom Jesus harshly rebuked became his most vocal adherents. Yet Jesus didn't walk around with a loaded verbal gun, ready to fire rebukes at anyone who demonstrated arrogance. On the contrary, he first built the kind of relationship with his disciples that would prepare them to profit from a stern rebuke.

Similarly, we must be certain that we have invested enough in a close professional or personal relationship to ensure that a rebuke will be profitable, even though it may be painful. In fact, our most pointed rebukes will likely be reserved for the people about whom we care the most. Remember that exhortations come wrapped in different kinds of packages. Sometimes, as Jesus demonstrated, they may be couched in the form of a rebuke.

None of us would say that we begin a course of action in order to see it fail miserably. Couples do not hurry to the church because they want to end up in divorce court. A businessman does not order a second martini at lunch because he wants to become an alcoholic. No one consumes huge desserts because he wants to binge his way into physical ruin. Yet these kinds of things happen to us every day because we do not have people in our lives who exhort us and lovingly rebuke us for our own good.

As leaders desiring to become more and more like the God who leads and inspires us, we simply must have those who will exhort us. Likewise, we must be willing to exhort others in order for them to realize their full potential.

PAUL AND THE ART OF EXHORTATION

Effective leaders accomplish extraordinary things by spurring others in the right way. By practicing the careful art of exhortation, they enable others to act. The apostle Paul demonstrated this ability in 2 Timothy 2:15–21:

> Do your best to present yourself to God as one approved, a workman who does not need to be ashamed and who correctly handles the word of truth. Avoid godless chatter, because those who indulge in it will become more and more ungodly. Their teaching will spread like gangrene. Among them are Hymenaeus and Philetus, who have wandered away from the truth. They say that the resurrection has already taken place, and they destroy the faith of some. Nevertheless, God's solid foundation stands firm, sealed with this inscription: "The Lord knows those who are his," and, "Everyone who confesses the name of the Lord must turn away from wickedness."
>
> In a large house there are articles not only of gold and silver, but also of wood and clay; some are for noble purposes and some for ignoble. If a man cleanses himself from the latter, he will be an

> instrument for noble purposes made holy, useful to
> the Master and prepared to do any good work.

Paul began with a general exhortation for Timothy to "present [him]self to God as one approved" (v. 15). He then offered specific guidelines as to how Timothy could accomplish this objective through his study and teaching of God's Word and also through the development of godly character and good personal habits. Finally, Paul offered Timothy a negative illustration followed by a positive one: Timothy was not to be like Hymenaeus and Philetus, who had strayed from the truth. Instead, he was to be like a gold or silver vessel in a great house. That vessel, when kept clean and polished, would be used by the Master for a noble purpose.

Timothy, being somewhat of a fearful and uncertain young man, lacked the level of godly self-confidence he needed to accomplish what he had been sent to Ephesus to do. Paul, demonstrating the qualities of a good mentor, encouraged and spurred Timothy on to higher levels of engagement than he otherwise might have pursued. A good mentor will see potential in another person and desire to bring that potential to its fulfillment.

Some of us are willing to settle for mediocrity. We all have times when we choose the good but not the best, when we do things well but not necessarily with excellence. This natural tendency is further complicated by the fact that our ability to live in self-deception is truly remarkable. Such self-deception, writes Neil Plantinga, is a strange and mysterious process that involves our willingness to pull the wool over our own eyes:

> We deny, suppress, or minimize what we know to
> be true. We assert, adorn, and elevate what we
> know to be false. We prettify ugly realities and sell
> ourselves the prettified versions. Thus a liar might
> transform "I tell a lot of lies to shore up my pride"
> to "Occasionally I finesse the truth in order to spare
> other people's feelings."[11]

We all need people who are willing and able to tell us the truth about ourselves. Only when we are willing and able to receive their exhortation are we competent and qualified to do the same for others.

Effective leaders, like Paul, use a variety of communication techniques to exhort those around them to strive for higher levels of performance. In so doing, they enable those whose lives they touch to be better prepared for their own leadership roles. The same will be true for us as chosen leaders of God's people.

1. Aristotle, *Nicomachean Ethics*, 8.1.
2. C. S. Lewis, *The Problem of Pain* (New York: Macmillan, 1940), 93.
3. M. Scott Peck, *The Different Drum* (New York: Simon & Schuster, 1987), 87ff.
4. Dietrich Bonhoeffer, *Life Together*, trans. Daniel Bloesch and James Burtness (Minneapolis: Fortress Press, 1996), 105.
5. John Ortberg, *Everybody's Normal Till You Get to Know Them* (Grand Rapids, MI: Zondervan, 2003), 179.
6. Warren Wiersbe, *Caring People* (Grand Rapids, MI: Baker Books, 2002), 103.
7. Bonhoeffer, *Life Together*, 105.
8. Dallas Willard, *The Divine Conspiracy* (San Francisco: HarperCollins, 1998), 218–21.
9. A. W. Tozer, *The Root of the Righteous* (Camp Hill, PA: Christian Publications, 1955), 17.
10. Ibid., 18.
11. Cornelius Plantinga Jr., *Not the Way It's Supposed to Be: A Breviary of Sin* (Grand Rapids, MI: Eerdmans, 1995), 105.

CHAPTER 15

Building Relationships

LEADERSHIP AND RELATIONSHIP

The value of people skills in the workplace can hardly be overstated. Zig Ziglar, for example, has said that according to Cavett Robert,

> Fifteen percent of the reason [people] get a job, keep that job and move ahead in that job, is determined by [their] technical skill and knowledge—regardless of their profession.... What about the other 85 percent? Cavett quotes Stanford Research Institute, Harvard University and the Carnegie Foundation as having proved that 85 percent of the reason people get a job, keep that job, and move ahead in that job has to do with [their] people skills and people knowledge.[1]

That is impressive information. It underlines the importance of human relationships to our work. And if human relationships play such an important role at work, they are crucial to our role as leaders. After all, leadership is about people in relationships.

THE GOD OF RELATIONSHIPS

The Bible is all about relationships. The greatest theologians of church history have agreed on this point. Obviously, the first example would be Jesus. When he was asked to sum up the God-centered life, he said that it was quite simple. Love God; love others (Mark 12:28–31). Later, Augustine, the great theologian of the early church, observed that everything written in Scripture is meant to teach us how to love either God or our neighbor.[2] More than a thousand years later, a converted Augustinian monk named Martin Luther echoed this same thought when he declared that the entire Christian life consists of relating to people around us—particularly by serving our neighbor.[3] As Michael Wittmer says, "The one truth that everyone seems to agree on, from Moses through Jesus and on to Augustine and the Reformers, is that it's virtually impossible to please God without loving our neighbors."[4]

Of course, this truth comes as no surprise when we consider that the triune God is a personal being who exists as a joyous community of humility, servanthood, and mutual submission. The Trinity is "a self-sufficing community of unspeakable magnificent personal beings of boundless love, knowledge and power," as Dallas Willard puts it.[5]

Not only does this great God exist in a perfect community himself, he has also paid a great price to make it possible for us to enter a relationship with him through the merits of Jesus Christ and the indwelling of the Holy Spirit. Of course, this is all an old, old story. Unfortunately, in our day, this familiar story has lost some of its power and punch; some of the mystery and wonder have worn off. And yet it is the single most magnificent story in all the world. There is nothing like it. God in his mercy and wisdom, fully understanding that we cannot save ourselves, initiates our salvation. He freely offers forgiveness to all those who will accept his simple invitation. Pardon and reconciliation are ours for the taking.

He wants this relationship, in turn, to be made visible in our relationships with others. God knows that not only are we unable to save ourselves, but we are also incapable of truly loving others. So, God goes beyond merely offering us salvation; when we accept his invitation, he miraculously infuses us with the ability to love others properly.

The apostle John affirms that God's love for us precedes our love for him and our love for people. God demonstrated his love for humanity in very tangible ways throughout the history of Israel, but he did so most fully and clearly in the redemptive work of Jesus Christ. This love is expressed not only in words, but also in actions. John says,

> This is how God showed his love among us: He sent his one and only Son into the world that we might live through him. This is love: not that we loved God, but that he loved us and sent his Son as an atoning sacrifice for our sins. Dear friends, since God so loved us, we also ought to love one another. (1 John 4:9–11)

God never simply says he loves us; he demonstrates it. To show his love, he gives. A genuine love will always be a generous love. God's love for us, agape love, is the steady intention of his will for our highest good. It is this agape love that he calls and enables us to extend toward others.

This sentiment is so strong in the mind of the Holy Spirit that later in the same chapter John tells us that those who do not love the members of God's family should seriously question whether they really love God (vv. 20–21). In other words, whatever begins with a love of God will inevitably end with a practical demonstration of love of neighbor.

There is a reciprocal relationship between loving God and loving people. "Everyone who believes that Jesus is the Christ is born of God, and everyone who loves the father loves his child as well. This is how we know that we love the children of God: by loving God and carrying out his commands" (1 John 5:1–2).

And what are his commands? Remember how Jesus answered that question: Love God; love others.

The religious leaders during Jesus' time had 613 laws that served as commentary on the Law of Moses. Much of Moses' codified law was commentary on the Ten Commandments. The Ten Commandments in turn can be easily divided between those that deal with our relationship to God and those that deal with our relationship to others. Thus, Jesus takes all of the commentaries and distills them into two overarching principles: Love God; love others. In the final analysis, the one who loves is the one who fulfills the Law. God is love, and he invites us to become lovers as well—not in words only, but in practical, tangible ways.

In fact, the importance of proper relationships is so central that in Scripture righteousness is not merely a legal status; it is, rather, a relational concept, since it refers to good, just, and loving associations with God and others. Righteousness is "right relationships" in the sense that it means being rightly related to God and others.

There is a line from the musical *Les Misérables* that sounds like what John is getting at: "To love another person is to see the face of God." We should think for a moment about the quality of our relationships. Are we pursuing any aspirations, ambitions, or accomplishments that threaten the quality of the relationships in our life? At the end of their lives, the things that people generally regret have far more to do with unfinished relational business than with uncompleted tasks. What must we do now to guarantee that we can look back at the end of our journey with no regrets?

TWO WAYS OF LIVING

Forgiveness and reconciliation often run counter to the way of the world and the way of our own hearts. God created us in his image—with the ability to connect with others in deep and meaningful ways. Yet it did not take long for us to learn how to disconnect and live as enemies. God created relational beings, beautiful and good. Shortly thereafter humans added a creation of their own: revenge (Genesis 4:1–8). Pain, betrayal, and loss are inevitable in a fallen world. But there are two ways to live in such a world: the way of revenge and the way of reconciliation. One road leads to death; the other road leads to life. On this subject Anne Lamott wrote,

> I went around saying for a long time that I am not one of those Christians who is heavily into forgiveness—that I am one of the other kind. But even though it was funny, and actually true, it started to be too painful to stay this way…. In fact, not forgiving is like drinking rat poison and waiting for the rat to die.[6]

Great leaders are well acquainted with forgiveness. The more we grasp the level of our own forgiveness, the easier it will be for us to forgive others.

Two Is Always Better than One

April 26, 2003, started out like a normal Saturday for Aron Ralston, a twenty-seven-year-old avid outdoorsman and mountain climber. Aron planned to spend the day riding his mountain bike and climbing rocks just outside Canyonlands National Park in southeastern Utah. As was his usual custom, Ralston planned to climb alone.

After a fifteen-mile bike ride to the Bluejohn Canyon trailhead, he locked his bike to a juniper tree and, dressed in a T-shirt and shorts and carrying a backpack, began to climb and hike his way toward Horseshoe Canyon. His backpack contained two burritos, less than a liter of water, a cheap pocketknife, a small first-aid kit, a video camera, a digital camera, and some rock climbing gear.

About 150 yards above the final rappel, Ralston was

maneuvering in a three-foot-wide slot trying to get over the top of a large boulder wedged between the narrow canyon walls. He scaled the boulder face and stood on top. It seemed very stable to him, but as he began to climb down the opposite side, the eight-hundred-pound rock shifted, pinning his right arm. Finding his pocketknife, he chipped away at the rock for ten hours, managing to produce only a small handful of dust. His arm was still trapped.

Sunday came and went. Monday passed. He was still trapped. He ran out of food and water on Tuesday. On Wednesday, he recorded a video message to his parents. He scored his name in the rock wall along with his birth date and what he was certain would be the date of his death. He finished his carving with three letters: R.I.P.

Sometime on Thursday morning, Ralston began hallucinating. He had a vision of a small boy running across a sunlit floor to be scooped up by a one-armed man. Something in his mind clicked, and he prepared to amputate his right arm below the elbow using his pocketknife. First, he broke the bones in his arm. Next he applied a tourniquet to his arm. He then used the knife blade to finish the procedure.

After applying some simple first aid, he rappelled nearly seventy feet to the bottom of Bluejohn Canyon and hiked five miles downstream into adjacent Horseshoe Canyon where he literally stumbled upon a Dutch family on vacation.

Meanwhile, back in Ralston's hometown of Aspen, Colorado, his friends began to worry when he failed to appear for work. Not only had Aron gone alone, he had also neglected to notify anyone of his itinerary.

Eventually, Aron Ralston was carried by helicopter to Allen Memorial Hospital in Moab, Utah, where he was treated for shock. His arm could not be reattached. A tragic event, to be sure, with a somewhat happy ending—Aron Ralston survived, but he paid a tremendous price.

Perhaps the most tragic part is that it all might have been avoided if Aron had taken someone else along with him. It is difficult to imagine a more poignant illustration of the biblical wisdom found in Ecclesiastes 4:9–10: "Two are better than one, because they have a good return for their work: If one falls down, his friend can help him up. But pity the man who falls and has no one to help him up!" This passage reminds us why we bring people together in organizations. We can not only do better work, we can help each other in difficult times.

In explaining this concept, the author of Ecclesiastes provides us with a powerful visual image: "Though one may be overpowered, two can defend themselves. A cord of three strands is not quickly broken" (4:12). Take a thread and see how much strength is needed to break it. It is easily doable. But take three strands of the same thread and twist them together; the task of snapping them becomes significantly more difficult. What is so simple with thread can be difficult in a leadership situation. Leaders must relate with their followers in a way that encourages the intertwining of ideas, commitments, and values.

Three separate individuals are as vulnerable as one individual alone. The word "relationship" implies the attempt to twist the threads together. The result? Better work, less vulnerability.

The two extremes to be avoided are codependence and independence. The balance to strive for is interdependence. The truth is, we must not base our identities upon another person. Neither should we think we can go through the toils and snares of life alone. As John Donne said, "No man is an island." We're not to go through life alone. Rather, we are called to enter into covenant relationships, walking together with others in peace and truth and mutual support.

HOSEA AND HIS UNFAITHFUL WIFE

Sometimes strengthening relationships requires both the grace of God and a deep reservoir of love. That was certainly the case with Hosea, who lived in Israel during a time of financial prosperity but spiritual poverty. God, through Hosea, called

Israel's failed leaders to account. They were wicked, deceptive, and arrogant. Because they had failed to acknowledge God, they—and their people—were doomed. As a prophet to Israel, Hosea's unenviable job was to predict the nation's exile and later restoration.

God is altogether righteous and lovingly jealous, yet he never disciplines simply out of anger. His discipline is always tempered by his mercy. So, in order to illustrate God's love for the nation of Israel, he commanded Hosea to marry a prostitute. Hosea did so, choosing a woman named Gomer to be his wife, and the not-surprising result was that his heart was broken when she proved unfaithful and eventually left him (Hosea 1:2). Later, at God's command Hosea sought out an emotionally broken and financially destitute Gomer, forgave her, and renewed their marriage relationship (3:1–2).

Through his marital problems, Hosea experienced something of God's grief for his unfaithful people. Hosea's love for Gomer serves as a picture of God's love for us—a love that is unconditional but also marked by his holiness. For our specific purposes here, however, Hosea serves as an example for us to follow. At times, each of us is called upon by God to seek out, forgive, and restore those who have wronged us. This amounts to nothing more than becoming like our Father in heaven. God forgives. But forgiveness never comes cheap. Such actions require that we grow in our ability to show the grace and love of God to those who hurt us and that we give up the right to hurt them in return.

Relationships and Real Wealth

"I may not have much money, but I'm filthy rich in relationships." The person who made this statement had his priorities in order, because he understood the true value of things on this earth. There is an enormous difference between loving things and using people and loving people and using things.

First Kings 19:19–21 marks a permanent transition in the lives of two men: Elijah and Elisha:

> So Elijah went from there and found Elisha son of
> Shaphat. He was plowing with twelve yoke of oxen,
> and he himself was driving the twelfth pair. Elijah
> went up to him and threw his cloak around him.
> Elisha then left his oxen and ran after Elijah. "Let me
> kiss my father and mother good-by," he said, "and
> then I will come with you."
> "Go back," Elijah replied. "What have I done to
> you?"
> So Elisha left him and went back. He took his
> yoke of oxen and slaughtered them. He burned the
> plowing equipment to cook the meat and gave it to
> the people, and they ate. Then he set out to follow
> Elijah and became his attendant.

When the old prophet Elijah approached the younger man
Elisha and threw his cloak around him, they both knew that
their lives would never again be the same. Elijah had become a
mentor, and Elisha his disciple. David Roper highlights the
weight of this encounter: "It is highly significant that [Elisha's]
oxen, the yoke, and the wooden ploughshare—all implements
related to his past life—were consumed in a final feast with his
family and friends. In an odd mix of metaphors, he burned his
bridges and ate them!"[7]

As we noted with Hosea, serving as a prophet was about as
rough as it got in ancient Israel. A prophet traveled constantly
and served tirelessly for little or no pay, and the benefits package
didn't go into effect until after death! In spite of these
drawbacks, many men and women answered the call to proclaim
the Word of the Lord to people who usually didn't have
much interest in hearing it. Eventually, after completing years of
prophetic service, Elijah was told by God that the time had come
to pass the torch to his young successor Elisha.

Elisha, whose name means "my God is salvation," proved to
be a good student and a faithful friend who was more than
equipped for the task. When Elijah attempted to persuade Elisha

to stay behind for Elijah's final journey, the younger man refused, saying, "As surely as the LORD lives and as you live, I will not leave you" (2 Kings 2:1–6).

But it soon became apparent that it was God's will for Elijah to leave Elisha, so the mentor asked his apprentice, "Tell me, what can I do for you before I am taken from you?" Elisha may have felt inadequate in comparison to the aged prophet, because he asked for a "double portion" of Elijah's spirit in order to carry out the work Elijah had begun (v. 9).

The Old Testament law stipulated that the older, favored brother was to receive a double share of his father's inheritance (Deuteronomy 21:17). Elisha was the "favored son" with respect to the ministry of Elijah, and, when he asked for a double portion of Elijah's spirit, this unusual request was honored (2 Kings 2:9–15).

Like Elijah, Elisha was obedient to God, eager to follow in the footsteps of his mentor. God granted Elisha's request, and Elijah left his cloak behind as a symbol of authority for the young prophet (2 Kings 2:11–13). Elisha ministered during the reigns of five different kings of Israel, and Scripture records twenty different miracles Elisha performed, including one that he performed after he was dead and buried (2 Kings 13:20–21).

Hundreds of years later, along the banks of the same river, there would be another, far more significant "passing of the mantle" as Jesus was baptized by John the Baptist, signaling the beginning of Jesus' public ministry (Matthew 3:13–17). As God's own Son, Jesus more than met the requirements for the task. He was and is faithful, never straying from his mission of doing the Father's will, performing it perfectly to the smallest detail (John 17:4).

The Elijah/Elisha association was also similar to Jesus' mentoring relationship with his disciples. Like Elisha, they had to drop everything and be willing to follow Jesus wherever he went. But they soon discovered that by loving Jesus more than others, they gained not only a greater ability to perform mighty works but also a greater capacity to love others.

Elisha and the disciples learned that following God's will is worth infinitely more than money. Jesus emphasized that truth when he told the Pharisees, who loved money, that "What is highly valued among men is detestable in God's sight" (Luke 16:15). Money and achievements will disappear in the end, but relationships will endure forever. This is why our Lord said, "I tell you, use worldly wealth to gain friends for yourselves, so that when it is gone, you will be welcomed into eternal dwellings" (Luke 16:9).

Relationships are the currency of God's kingdom. The one who wins in life is not the one who has the most toys, but the one who has the best relationships.

IS IT REAL?

Many years ago—it was May of 1986, though it seems like only yesterday—I was ministering at a men's retreat, and a friend of mine named Paul was going through a very difficult time. His father had recently died, and as a new believer Paul needed encouragement. As we drove to the airport he asked me a question: "Is it real?" In other words, "Is all this really true? Is there life beyond what we can see and feel and taste and touch? Should I really bank on these things?" I suppose Paul asked me these hard questions because he respected me and knew that I would tell him the truth.

I can remember everything about that moment—where he was standing, what he was wearing, how he searched my face for assurance. I looked him in the eye and said, "Paul, it's real."

Some years later I received a call from Paul. He was doing well financially, spiritually, and relationally. But he was struggling with direction, struggling with what God was calling him to do and to be. He said, "You know, I guess I want to hear you say that again, that it's real."

It is such an honor to be chosen by God to assist people in

these holy moments. That is what mentoring is often about, the giving and receiving of encouragement, the knowledge that there is someone who believes in us, who loves us, and who will tell us, "Yes, it is real."

None of us can go through life alone, because sooner or later we all fall down. Usually we have enough inner strength to pick ourselves back up again. But the time comes for all of us when we fall and find that we cannot go on. It is in those times that we discover our true need for others, our real need for relationship.

1. Zig Ziglar, *Top Performance* (New York: Berkeley Books, 1986), 11.
2. Augustine, "Sermon 350: On Charity," in *The Works of Saint Augustine: A Translation for the 21st Century III*, vol. 3, no. 10, ed. John E. Rotelle, trans. Edmund Hill (New York: New City Press, 1995), 108.
3. Martin Luther, "The Freedom of a Christian," in *Luther's Works,* 31, ed. Harold J. Grimm and Helmut T. Lehmann (Philadelphia: Muhlenberg Press, 1957), 365.
4. Michael Wittmer, *Heaven Is a Place on Earth* (Grand Rapids, MI: Zondervan, 2004), 102.
5. Dallas Willard, *The Divine Conspiracy* (San Francisco: HarperSanFrancisco, 1998), 318.
6. Anne Lamott, *Traveling Mercies* (New York: Doubleday/Anchor, 2000), 128, 134.
7. David Roper, *Seeing Through* (Sisters, OR: Multnomah, 1995), 200.

CHAPTER 16

Servant Leadership

SELF-SACRIFICE FOR TEAM SUCCESS

One of professional sports' most legendary coaches, Pat Riley has motivated, taught, and inspired his way up the NBA managerial ranks. He exemplifies what it means to be a leader, and athletes and businessmen alike could all learn something from this accomplished basketball mind. The driving force behind the Los Angeles Lakers' memorable "Showtime" era, Riley took Magic Johnson, Kareem Abdul-Jabbar, and the rest of the high-flying team to four NBA titles in nine years. He is the second-winningest coach in NBA history and the fastest manager in any of the four major professional sports to reach one thousand wins. In his book *The Winner Within*, the outstanding NBA coach wrote about the "danger of me":

> The most difficult thing for individuals to do when they're part of the team is to sacrifice. It's so easy to become selfish in a team environment. To play for me. It's very vulnerable to drop your guard and say, "This is who I am and I'm gonna open up and give of myself to you." But that's exactly what you've got to do. Willingness to sacrifice is the great paradox. You must give up something in the immediate present—

comfort, ease, recognition, quick rewards—to attract
something even better in the future.[1]

What Riley said about the basketball court is also true in life.
Serving others can be tough; expending energies and resources
in the interest of others can be exhausting. Yet the most effective leaders are servants.

THE SERVANT LEADER

While much is being said these days about servant leadership,
it is far from a new concept. In fact, we can find its roots
deeply imbedded in the Bible. From Genesis to Revelation we see
a steady stream of leaders who used their position and power for
the greater good of those around them. Clearly, nobody demonstrated this principle better than Jesus of Nazareth, and there is no
time he more clearly modeled the virtue of servant leadership
than on the night prior to his crucifixion.

As the disciples entered the upper room, they got into a little argument about their prospective positions. The fuss was
likely kindled by disagreement about who was to sit closest to
Jesus. Undoubtedly they neglected Jesus' six-month-old advice
to the Pharisees about sitting in the lowest positions rather than
elbowing one's way up the table (Luke 14:7–11).

Jesus had just given a verbal response to the disciples' debate
about who was the greatest (Luke 22:24–30). Next came his
visual response. He said that he came as one who served and not
as one who sat at the table (v. 27). The astonished disciples then
learned the truth of these words. Alone with his disciples in a
room in Jerusalem, Jesus did the unthinkable. While the disciples settled into their respective cushions and the Passover meal
was being served, Jesus unpretentiously rose from the table and
wrapped himself with a towel.

The evening meal was being served.... Jesus knew

that the Father had put all things under his power,
and that he had come from God and was returning to
God; so he got up from the meal, took off his outer
clothing, and wrapped a towel around his waist. After
that, he poured water into a basin and began to wash
his disciples' feet, drying them with the towel that
was wrapped around him. (John 13:2–5)

When there was no servant to carry out the customary task
of foot washing, Jesus assumed the role. The Master became the
servant. The greatest and highest became the least and the lowest. In one stunning act, Jesus demonstrated that in the
kingdom of God, service is not the path to greatness; service *is*
greatness. Here the divine perspective shines through and
appears to our disoriented minds to be upside down.

Author M. Scott Peck was so struck by this scene that he
counted it as one of the most significant events of Jesus' life:

Until that moment the whole point of things had
been for someone to get on top, and once he had
gotten on top to stay on top or else attempt to get
farther up. But here this man already on top—who
was rabbi, teacher, master—suddenly got down on
bottom and began to wash the feet of his followers.
In that one act Jesus symbolically overturned the
whole social order. Hardly comprehending what was
happening, even his own disciples were almost horri-
fied by his behavior.[2]

Jesus was able to assume the position of servant because he
was secure in himself. He knew who he was, where he had
come from, and where he was going. But Jesus also served his
disciples because he loved them. The first verse of the chapter
says, "Having loved his own who were in the world, he now
showed them the full extent of his love." While these two reasons would be adequate in and of themselves, the Lord had
another reason for his actions.

> When he had finished washing their feet, he put on
> his clothes and returned to his place. "Do you under-
> stand what I have done for you?" he asked them.
> "You call me 'Teacher' and 'Lord,' and rightly so, for
> that is what I am. Now that I, your Lord and Teacher,
> have washed your feet, you also should wash one
> another's feet. I have set you an example that you
> should do as I have done for you. I tell you the truth,
> no servant is greater than his master, nor is a mes-
> senger greater than the one who sent him. Now that
> you know these things, you will be blessed if you do
> them." (John 13:12–17)

The Lord didn't tell them to do "what" he had done. He commanded them to do "as" he had done. They weren't to become
full-time foot washers, but rather full-time servants of men and
women. They were to be servant leaders. John Calvin was right
in saying, "Christ does not enjoin an annual ceremony here, but
tells us to be ready, all through our life, to wash the feet of our
brethren."[3] Far from meaning that we are to wash feet literally,
Christ means for us to live a life of love, and of humble and sac-
rificial service.

The act of washing feet certainly does not hold the same
cultural significance for us as it did for those in the first century. So while foot washing may be a humbling gesture and a
beautiful religious act, today we can easily miss the pragmatic
significance it had for the apostles. Jesus calls us, not to a single act but to a single attitude that may manifest itself in many
different ways. In our day it might mean taking out the trash,
cleaning bathrooms, or changing diapers. "Foot washing"
translates into performing lowly tasks that everyone else
avoids because of pride.

Notice that Jesus never calls us to do something that he
hasn't already done for us. Just as he doesn't call us to love others without having loved us, or forgive others without having
forgiven us, neither does he invite us to serve others without

having already served us. Having loved, forgiven, and served us, he now invites us to participate in the ministry of the towel alongside him.

In his book *The God of the Towel*, Jim McGuiggan outlines the secret of Jesus' power and ability to surrender:

> The Scripture tells us [Jesus] had a number of things on his mind. Telling us over and over what "Jesus knew," John wants the reader to understand that Christ does what he does in light of his knowing and loving.
>
> Jesus knew that the hour he had come into the world to meet had finally arrived—the hour of betrayal, the hour of incredible inner turmoil, the hour of national rejection and sin-bearing.
>
> Jesus knew that the Father had unchangeably purposed to give all authority and control to him— authority beyond the wildest dreams of the greatest megalomaniac.
>
> Jesus knew that he had come out from God—he was fully aware of his divine origin. He had under-stood this even as a twelve-year-old boy, and a short but full life had not shaken that conviction—rather, it had strengthened it.
>
> Jesus knew he was going back to the Father—this was his divine destination. He knew he faced treach-ery, humiliation, desertion, and the Cross, but he also knew that he would return to glory with his Father.[4]

God has gone to great lengths to provide a basis for us to know our security, identity, and destiny. In the Bible we read that nothing can separate those of us who are in Christ from the love of God (Romans 8:38–39). We also read that those of us who have surrendered to this great love of God are now the children of God (1 John 3:1). Finally, the Bible assures us that as children of God, we will one day be taken away to be with Jesus in the Father's house forever (John 14:2–3).

The Suffering Leader

More often than not, leadership skills are used in the service of personal gain and career advancement rather than in the service of others. Yet God himself demonstrated, through the life and ministry of his Son, that leadership is intended for use in an *others*-centered way.

In ancient religions it was commonplace for people to offer sacrifices to the gods, but the notion that a god would make a sacrifice for humanity was almost beyond imagination. The Jewish people themselves had no such concept despite the fact that their own Scriptures predicted it. This is the reason that Jesus, after his resurrection, rebuked two of his disciples on the road to Emmaus: "How foolish you are, and how slow of heart to believe all that the prophets have spoken! Did not the Christ have to suffer these things and then enter his glory?" (Luke 24:25–26). Since the Jews were looking for a powerful Messiah who would deliver them from their bondage to Rome, they overlooked the prophecies about the Suffering Servant who would deliver them from the greater bondage to sin and guilt:

> See, my servant will act wisely; he will be raised and
> lifted up and highly exalted. Just as there were many
> who were appalled at him—his appearance was so
> disfigured beyond that of any man and his form
> marred beyond human likeness—so will he sprinkle
> many nations, and kings will shut their mouths
> because of him. For what they were not told, they
> will see, and what they have not heard, they will
> understand. (Isaiah 52:13–15)

Written seven hundred years before Jesus was born, this passage—actually the first stanza of a poem—reveals the unlikely path to glory that Jesus, the Suffering Servant, would take. In this initial portion, we find a description of the *program* of God's Servant. The poem then moves on to describe the *person* of God's Servant:

Who has believed our message and to whom has the
arm of the LORD been revealed? He grew up before
him like a tender shoot, and like a root out of dry
ground. He had no beauty or majesty to attract us to
him, nothing in his appearance that we should desire
him. He was despised and rejected by men, a man of
sorrows, and familiar with suffering. Like one from
whom men hide their faces he was despised, and we
esteemed him not. (Isaiah 53:1–3)

Here we see clearly an image of rejection. Jesus was the root,
planted by God, who grew up in the dry soil of Israel's rejection
and isolationism and religious legalism. Far from being sent to a
receptive audience, Jesus came to his own, only to be rejected
by them (John 1:11). Naturally, this rejection leads to the
poem's next stanza—this time dealing with the Servant's *passion*:

Surely he took up our infirmities and carried our sorrows, yet we considered him stricken by God,
smitten by him, and afflicted. But he was pierced for
our transgressions, he was crushed for our iniquities;
the punishment that brought us peace was upon
him, and by his wounds we are healed. We all, like
sheep, have gone astray, each of us has turned to his
own way; and the LORD has laid on him the iniquity
of us all. (vv. 4–6)

This One, who suffered so unjustly at the hands of wicked
and perverse men, could have justly demanded his rights. We
almost expect him to do so. But the depths of our Savior's love
are only compounded by what we read about next—the *patience*
of God's Servant:

He was oppressed and afflicted, yet he did not open
his mouth; he was led like a lamb to the slaughter,
and as a sheep before her shearers is silent, so he did
not open his mouth. By oppression and judgment he

> was taken away. And who can speak of his descen-
> dants? For he was cut off from the land of the living;
> for the transgression of my people he was stricken.
> He was assigned a grave with the wicked, and with
> the rich in his death, though he had done no vio-
> lence, nor was any deceit in his mouth. (vv. 7–9)

So, the question rings in every thinking and feeling person's ears: Why? The section ends with a description of the *provision* of God's Suffering Servant:

> Yet it was the LORD's will to crush him and cause him
> to suffer, and though the LORD makes his life a guilt
> offering, he will see his offspring and prolong his
> days, and the will of the LORD will prosper in his
> hand. After the suffering of his soul, he will see the
> light of life and be satisfied; by his knowledge my
> righteous servant will justify many, and he will bear
> their iniquities. Therefore I will give him a portion
> among the great, and he will divide the spoils with
> the strong, because he poured out his life unto death,
> and was numbered with the transgressors. For he
> bore the sin of many, and made intercession for the
> transgressors. (vv. 10–12)

The heart of the prophecy is in the third section, which describes the Servant's "passion" or suffering. Isaiah told us (using the past tense) that the Suffering Servant "took up our infirmities and carried our sorrows" (v. 4). The Hebrew word for "took up" connotes lifting something and carrying it away. Jesus *took up* our sin, and the necessary punishment, and carried them away (1 Peter 2:24). Recognizing our Savior's death for what it was means viewing his act of love as taking God's righteous judgment on *himself* for our sake (Romans 5:6–11). Isaiah referred to the Messiah as "stricken" by God for our sin (Isaiah 53:4).

In another graphic image Isaiah stated that God's Son was

"pierced for our transgressions" (Isaiah 53:5). The Hebrew word here means "pierced through," carrying the connotation of violent and excruciating torture. We can also recognize the reference to crucifixion—Jesus' hands and feet were literally "pierced through" with nails as he hung on the cross (John 20:25; Acts 2:23; cf. John 19:34).

Isaiah also used an agricultural term, saying that Jesus was (or would be) "crushed" for our iniquities (Isaiah 53:5), like harvested grapes trampled in a vat until they burst and the juice is released. In the "winepress" of God's wrath (Revelation 14:19), Jesus was crushed until his spirit was broken (Psalm 34:18) and his blood was shed in atonement for our sin (Romans 3:25).

Jesus assumed God's punishment for our sin so that we could have peace with the Father (Romans 5:1; Ephesians 2:14–18; Colossians 1:19–20). Punishment and peace strike us as a strange combination. But it is only because Jesus was punished for our sin that we are restored to fellowship with the holy God and granted *shalom*—the Hebrew word for the peace for which God's people had waited for centuries.

Finally, in verse 5 we see that we are *healed* because Jesus was *wounded*. This beautiful passage in Isaiah 53 includes a reminder of the desperate human condition that required Jesus to undergo such suffering: We are like sheep, lost and in rebellion against God. Verse 6 both begins and ends with a collective reference to all people. "We all" were lost—but God has laid on Jesus' shoulders the weight of the sin of "us all." But Jesus' suffering would not be the end of his story. Isaiah pointed, this time in the future tense, beyond the anguish of the cross: "After the suffering of his soul, [Jesus] will see the light of life and be satisfied; by his knowledge my righteous servant will justify many, and he will bear their iniquities" (v. 11).

Jesus is the perfect fulfillment of Old Testament prophecy. As the Suffering Servant of Isaiah, Jesus clearly communicated his purpose for coming to this earth: "For even the Son of Man did not come to be served, but to serve, and to give his life as a ransom for many" (Mark 10:45). In his sacrifice on the cross, Jesus provides us with the ultimate illustration of servant leadership. Jesus did not suffer on our behalf *in spite of* his identity but, rather, *precisely because of* his identity. Service and sacrifice were part of his very nature. Thus, in calling us to become like himself, he calls us to join him in a lifestyle of service and sacrifice. Such service and sacrifice is not to be done *in spite of* our positions of leadership but, rather, *precisely because of* our positions of leadership.

His example of servanthood transcends any that has ever been seen, before or since: "You see, at just the right time, when we were still powerless, Christ died for the ungodly. Very rarely will anyone die for a righteous man, though for a good man someone might possibly dare to die. But God demonstrates his own love for us in this: While we were still sinners, Christ died for us" (Romans 5:6–8).

THE SECURE LEADER

Like Jesus, we may be secure in our identity and destiny. In fact, it is only to the extent we grasp these same concepts that we will be able to serve others as Christ did. On the other hand, the more insecure we are in our true identity and eternal destiny, the more likely we are to manipulate people in a desperate attempt to get our needs met.

Others-centered leadership, having been clearly modeled for us in the life of Jesus, is now our premier calling. We are called, now, not to be served in this world, but to serve and to give our lives away. Thus, by losing our lives, we will discover them in their truest sense.

Taking on a servant role will quickly squelch a competitive spirit. A servant mind-set compels us to involve ourselves in the mundane and disagreeable tasks of everyday life. We often like to set our sights on the big and impressive tasks we desire to undertake. But living as Jesus lived means serving others in the seemingly insignificant areas too. It may mean stopping along the roadside to help someone change a tire, purchasing a cup of lemonade from a child's sidewalk stand, allowing the busy mother with an armful of groceries to move ahead of us in the line, and countless other "random acts of kindness." Jesus advised his disciples that deferring to the needs of others in such seemingly trivial ways demonstrates respect for God and will be rewarded (Mark 9:41). Our Lord's gracious rewards are given to those who serve him as they offer themselves to others in simple, yet profound, ways.

THE COUNTER-CULTURAL LEADER

A t some point in the future, every knee will bow at the name of Jesus (Philippians 2:9–11). In a true sense, then, the question is not "*Will* we acknowledge Jesus as Lord?" but rather "*When* will we acknowledge Jesus as Lord?" Yet Jesus came to earth in the form of a servant, and he expects those of us who serve him in this world to express that service to him through our ministry to others. Following the model of our Savior, we are called to be willing to give up our rights and position in this life and live in a way that will enable others to experience God's love.

A biblical view of servant leadership makes evident the fact that the service we render to others is really a measure of the service we render to God. Christ himself is the model of this servant mind-set, and he commands us to imitate his service to them. Thus, putting ourselves in the position of a servant brings us forward in our goal of becoming more Christlike. Jesus certainly had every right to be served by all of creation, yet he chose to be a servant throughout his earthly life and ultimately to die for our sin. And he asks each of us to follow his servant model: "Whoever wants to become great among you must be your servant, and whoever wants to be first must be slave of all" (Mark 10:43–44).

On more than one occasion, Jesus' disciples argued about

"which of them was considered to be greatest" (Luke 22:24; cf. Matthew 20:20–28). As they jockeyed for the highest position in the kingdom, Jesus had to encourage them to turn their thinking upside down. He informed them that the way of God's children must be radically different from the way of this world. Few statements Jesus made could be considered as counter-cultural as this one. Earthly rulers seek power and control, but for the followers of Christ, "If anyone wants to be first, he must be the very last, and the servant of all" (Mark 9:35).

The Influential Leader

As we have seen, while the concept of servant leadership has recently become very popular it is by no means new. Jesus required it as a foundational character trait of any who would follow him. Dr. Frank Davey has written:

> Jesus reversed the social priorities of his day by demonstrating and teaching a special concern for the poor, the disabled, the outcast and the underprivileged. Such people had no special claim to attention until Jesus became their champion.... One cannot imagine Hippocrates showing much interest in a prostitute in trouble, a blind beggar, the slave of a soldier of the occupying power, a psychotic foreigner clearly with no money, an old woman with a chronic spinal condition. Jesus not only did so, he expected his followers to do the same.[5]

But Jesus didn't merely talk about serving others; he was—and is—the ultimate model of one who serves. Now, as when he walked on earth, Jesus serves those he leads.

Jesus is deserving of our complete and uninhibited worship because he is God the Son. In Revelation 5:11–12 the apostle John heard in his vision the incredible sounds of thousands of angel voices lifted together in song. The melody reached a spine-tingling crescendo and reverberated throughout the heavens: "Worthy is the Lamb, who was slain, to receive power and wealth and wisdom and strength and honor and glory and praise!" (v. 12). This angel host was soon joined by every other living creature, both in heaven and on earth, shouting out their praise: "To him who sits on the throne and to the Lamb be praise and honor and glory and power, for ever and ever!" (v. 13).

What exactly had Jesus done to deserve this adulation?

The scene opened with John grieving deeply because it appeared that no one would be able to deal with God's wrath against the sin of humanity, to break the seals, unveiling the mystery of the consummation of all history, and open God's scroll of judgment: "I wept and wept because no one was found who was worthy to open the scroll or look inside" (v. 4), wrote John. One of the elders present was quick to reassure the distraught apostle, however: "Do not weep! See, the Lion of the tribe of Judah, the Root of David, has triumphed. He is able to open the scroll and its seven seals" (v. 5).

At this point John looked up and perceived the Lamb of God (v. 6; cf. John 1:29), Jesus Christ, standing in the very center of the throne room, surrounded by citizens of heaven. Jesus reached out and accepted the scroll from his Father's hand. At that moment the four living creatures and the twenty-four elders who were with him broke forth into a new song: "You are worthy to take the scroll and to open its seals, because you were slain, and with your blood you purchased men for God from every tribe and language and people and nation" (v. 9).

Jesus is the Root of David, the Messiah whom God had promised to send into the world. He was willing to renounce his heavenly privilege for a time in order to come down to earth (Philippians 2:6–8) and offer himself as the atoning sacrifice for our sins (1 John 2:2). The book of Revelation provides us with a unique glimpse into the future, when Jesus Christ will reign forever as the righteous, eternal King over a renewed creation. Jesus is indeed deserving of our unqualified adoration and devotion. He is the One to whom we also can sing "a new song"

(Revelation 5:9) every day of our lives—and we will never run out of reasons to praise him.

The pages of human history are stained with the disastrous consequences experienced by people who have misused their privileges of power, wealth, exceptional intelligence, strength, or honor. From Samson to Solomon, our fallen race has been unable to use these gifts in ways that honor God and benefit others. But Jesus is different. He is not only worthy of all these wonderful gifts, but he also uses them to express his love for his Father (1 Corinthians 15:24) and his beloved children (2 Thessalonians 2:14).

The description of the exalted Jesus in Revelation 15 inspires awe in the thoughtful reader. What a magnificent picture of the supreme position held by the risen Christ! To refer to him merely as a "leader" might sound rather demeaning. But to call him a *servant?* Such a label might appear blasphemous—were it not for the fact that he went to such unspeakable lengths to achieve that very title.

Isaiah prophesied that Jesus, God's own Son, would be the Suffering Servant (Isaiah 53). And Jesus lived his life as the definitive statement about service as the path to greatness (Matthew 20:26–28). What's more, Paul identified Jesus as the ultimate example of servant leadership. He told the church in Philippi that, "Christ Jesus ... being in very nature God ... made himself nothing, taking the very nature of a servant" (Philippians 2:5–7).

It is absolutely correct to state that no one else has ever influenced the world as Jesus did ... and does ... and will. Bishop Stephen Neill asked this profound and thought-provoking question: "What kind of a stone could it be that, once thrown into the pool of human existence, could set in motion ripples that would go on spreading until the utmost rim of the world had been reached?"[6] John Stott appropriately answers the question:

> Only the incomparable Christ. And if we are prepared to take the risk of familiarizing ourselves with

his story, and exposing ourselves to his personality, example and teaching, we shall not remain unscathed. Rather we too shall feel the power of his influence and say with Paul that the love of Christ tightens its grip upon us, until we are left with no alternative but to live—and die—for him.[7]

The earliest followers of Jesus bore witness to this claim. John exalted him as the Lord of lords and King of kings (Revelation 17:14). Paul attested that "God exalted him to the highest place and gave him the name that is above every name" (Philippians 2:9).

Jesus led in such a way that no one who came into contact with him remained unchanged. In turn, he insisted that his followers lead as he did: by serving. No one could—or can—argue with his command, because he modeled the kind of service he was advocating. And he certainly models greatness. Jesus Christ is the ultimate servant leader.

THE SYMPATHETIC LEADER

In his exalted heavenly position, as in his humble earthly role, Jesus leads by serving. He sits at the Father's right hand, exalted above all other beings. Yet his concern and passion are for the good of his followers. He can sympathize with our weakness because he was willing to be tested as we are tested. He paid a terrible price so he can say, "Come boldly before my throne of grace. I understand. I've been where you are." In Hebrews the writer elaborates again on Jesus' tenacious pursuit of our good. This passage should be required reading for all leaders:

> In bringing many sons to glory, it was fitting that
> God, for whom and through whom everything
> exists, should make the author of their salvation
> perfect through suffering. Both the one who makes

men holy and those who are made holy are of the same family. So Jesus is not ashamed to call them brothers....

Since the children have flesh and blood, he too shared in their humanity so that by his death he might destroy him who holds the power of death—that is, the devil—and free those who all their lives were held in slavery by their fear of death. For surely it is not angels he helps, but Abraham's descendants. For this reason he had to be made like his brothers in every way, in order that he might become a merciful and faithful high priest in service to God, and that he might make atonement for the sins of the people. Because he himself suffered when he was tempted, he is able to help those who are being tempted....

Therefore, since we have a great high priest who has gone through the heavens, Jesus the Son of God, let us hold firmly to the faith we profess. For we do not have a high priest who is unable to sympathize with our weaknesses, but we have one who has been tempted in every way, just as we are—yet was without sin. Let us then approach the throne of grace with confidence, so that we may receive mercy and find grace to help us in our time of need. (Hebrews 2:10–11, 14–18; 4:14–16)

We should allow this passage to soak deeply into the very root of our beings. It is essential truth.

All of us who want to be great leaders must be willing to serve others to the best of our ability. A prolonged and concentrated meditation on the passage above will provide us an excellent starting point for shaping the values needed for genuine service. Each of us must allow the greatest servant leader the world will ever know to serve us by teaching us how to lead through service.

1. Pat Riley, *The Winner Within* (New York: Putnam Publishing Group, 1993), 53.
2. M. Scott Peck, *The Different Drum* (New York: Simon & Schuster, 1987), 293.
3. John Calvin, *The Gospel According to St. John 11–21* (Edinburgh: Oliver & Boyd, 1961), 60, comment on John 13:14.
4. Jim McGuiggan, *The God of the Towel,* (West Monroe, LA: Howard Publishing Company, 1997), 135–36.
5. S. G. Browne, T. F. Davey, and W. A. R. Thomson, eds., *Heralds of Health: The Sage of Christian Medical Initiatives* (London: Christian Medical Fellowship, 1985), 7.
6. S. C. Neill and N. T. Wright, *The Interpretation of the New Testament 1861–1986* (New York: Oxford University Press, 1988), 19.
7. John Stott, *The Incomparable Christ* (Downers Grove, IL: InterVarsity Press, 2001), 166.

READERS' GUIDE

for Personal Reflection or
Group Discussion

Readers' Guide

Obeying God's call to lead others is a marvelous and intimidating undertaking. Every leader enjoys, at times, the thrill of seeing his or her followers come to a deeper maturity and of seeing the tasks they are facing together find fulfillment; but each leader also feels the pain of failure and frustration when things do not go as planned.

The task of leadership is not to be taken lightly. Scripture says that "from everyone who has been given much, much will be demanded" (Luke 12:48). Leaders are given not just skills and opportunities, not just a cause and a calling (and those things are plentiful in themselves), but leaders are also given lives to shape and direct. It is an awesome responsibility. Thankfully, it is not a venture one needs to take on his or her own.

In C. S. Lewis' *Prince Caspian*, a child named Lucy encounters Aslan, the Christ-figure of the Narnia stories, after not seeing him for a long while. "Aslan, you're bigger," she says.

"That is because you're older, little one," answered he.

"Not because you are?"

"I am not. But every year you grow, you will find me bigger."[1]

The more mature in the faith we are, the bigger God will be for us. As our vision of God becomes clearer and we understand his enormity, we learn to rest in him. We grow in our ability to depend completely on him and know that with a God as competent as the God we find in the pages of Scripture, the universe in which we find ourselves is truly a safe place for us.

To grow in your ability as a godly leader, find a partner or a small group of people to study this book with. (Just don't fight over who gets to lead the group.) Use the following questions as a springboard for discussion.

CHAPTER 1

Would you consider integrity to be one of the top characteristics required in a leader? Why or why not? How have you seen this displayed (or neglected) in a leader you have followed? How did this leader's integrity (or lack of it) affect you?

Malachi 3:6 says, "I the LORD do not change." Can you name other Scripture passages or think of biblical stories that support the truth of this statement? Do you believe that God's consistency makes him the true example of integrity? Why or why not?

Have you found in your own life that God is a leader who can be trusted? What experiences have you had that bring you to the level of trust in your relationship with him?

Do you agree with the author's definition of integrity: an integration of beliefs and practice? Why or why not? What successes and failures have you experienced in this area? What steps can you take to continue to grow in integrity?

When Jesus confronted the leaders of his day (the Pharisees), he was far from gentle. What would Jesus say to you if he were walking the earth today? How would you respond?

Can you appreciate the beauty of Samuel's integrity: not one person rose up to make a claim against him even when he publicly offered to make amends for any injustice he had committed. What can you learn from him as you work to become the leader God has called you to be?

CHAPTER 2

If it's true that people delight to follow leaders with godly character and that godly character is formed by the pursuit of wisdom, why are so many leaders swayed by public opinion? Name some great leaders whose wisdom swayed the people rather than the other way around.

God does not leave us to guess his character; he states it for us clearly: "The LORD, the LORD, the compassionate and gracious God, slow to anger, abounding in love and faithfulness, maintaining love to thousands, and forgiving wickedness, rebellion and sin. Yet he does not leave the guilty unpunished; he punishes the children and their children for the sin of the fathers to the third and fourth generation" (Exodus 34:6–7). Is the God of the Bible a person of character whom you respect?

Respecting our leaders is one thing; loving them is the real test. Has the character of God, as revealed in his Word, in his world, and in your relationship with him, caused you to grow to love him? Why or why not?

Leaders are usually aware that they often serve as a role model to others. How have you been able to balance being authentic about your own failures while living up to the responsibility of modeling Christlike behavior to others?

Do you find it easy to slip into the habit of trying to be perfect by your own strength? Does it comfort you or bother you to know that you will never get it right? Why? Do you believe that the character you display flows from the work of the Spirit within you? How does that help or hinder you to be a person of character?

Does it comfort you to know that Peter, who messed up so terribly at the beginning of his walk with Christ, became one of the key leaders of the church? What can you learn from the mistakes he made?

CHAPTER 3

Even before the days when writing out a vision statement became popular, core values were the thing that drove great leaders. If you think of a leader you respect, would you be able to name the one or two core values he or she held? In other words, what is it that drove that person to action, even if he or she didn't realize it?

The Ten Commandments reveal the values of God. Read Exodus 20:1–17 and see if you can name some of the core values of God. How has God revealed himself to be the ultimate leader?

Do you agree with the author that "our notions of good and evil come to us because we bear the image of the One who initially determined the categories"? Do you know people (or have you been one of those people) who live out the core values God has designated for his people even before they come to know God? What does that teach you about God?

Have you ever taken the time to list your core values? If so, make sure that you review them on a regular basis so that you can challenge yourself to live them out. If not, spend some time in prayer and reflection as you begin this process.

Have you chosen your values based on what you believe others will approve of, or are your core values based on what God calls you to? How can you discern your own motivation and how can you take steps to change the things that resulted from improper motivation?

The apostle Paul knew how to prioritize. He was willing to give up anything that contradicted his values. What can you learn from Paul about knowing what matters and what doesn't?

CHAPTER 4

Leaders are often pressured to show great strength in their resolve, and so many are hesitant to change direction even when they know they've made a mistake. Can you think of any role models in your life who did change directions for the better? How did their willingness to be humble affect others?

Over and over, Scripture makes it clear that we cannot understand the ways of God, and yet it is just as clear that God has a passion and a purpose for his people. Do you think that God is ever weary of his choice to love us? Back up your answer with Scripture. What does his enduring faithfulness to his purpose and passion (intimacy with us!) tell you about God? about leadership?

Do you have a loving relationship with Christ? If so, what do you think your love for him does for God? If not, how do you think your rejection makes him feel? Why do you think God continues to pursue even those who reject him?

If passion is caring intensely about something, passion is also what drives a person to certain behaviors. Do you know what your passion is? How do the things you are passionate about determine your purpose for life and the way you lead others?

Does it matter what leaders are passionate about, or is it enough for them to have a lot of enthusiasm? Likewise, does the leader need a strategy to implement purpose, or is it enough to cast the vision? Do you have enthusiasm and strategy in regards to your purpose?

Once Paul met Jesus, he was passionate and single-minded in his desire for others to know this God. Do you admire his passion or does that kind of energy intimidate you? What would it take to find that kind of single-minded focus in your own leadership?

CHAPTER 5

Do you know any great leaders (public figures or unknown citizens) who do not realize the wonderful effect they have on others? Why do you think they are oblivious to their own greatness?

Scripture tells us that Jesus "humbled himself and became obedient to death—even death on a cross!" (Philippians 2:8). Why do you think God, the most powerful leader ever, would humble himself to the level of a servant? What does that tell you about God? about leadership?

Have you ever obeyed God even when you didn't understand or didn't agree with his plan? If so, what happened? If you disobeyed, what happened? Why is obeying God difficult even when we know that his plan is always better than our own?

We all want to be able to call ourselves humble, but are you genuinely glad when others treat you as a servant? Why or why not? How can you train yourself to be others-centered?

What does true humility mean to you? Do you believe you can have a sense of your own value and dignity when you are humble? Can you seek success even when you are humble? Why or why not?

Why do you think God said that Moses was the most humble man on the face of the earth? Does it comfort you to know that a great leader can be both courageous and fearful? Have you ever hesitated to be the leader God called you to be? What happened?

CHAPTER 6

Many people long to be a leader without realizing that the job description calls for much more nitty-gritty than glamorous work.

Can you think of any people who became leaders out of their commitment rather than their charisma? Why did people follow them?

Name the various ways that God commits himself to us as shown through Scripture. How does God's willingness to go all the way for his people change your understanding of leadership?

Have you experienced the commitment of God on a personal level? If so, how did you respond? If not, what can you do to move the beautiful truth from your head to your heart?

What is the one thing you are most committed to? If your answer is God, how does that play out in your life? If your answer is anything other than him, do you wish that you could honestly place him first in your life? Why or why not?

Do you believe that if you seek first the kingdom of God, the other things you want and need will fall into place? Why or why not?

Do you think you have the perseverance to place God first in your life *all* your life, as Joshua did? Why or why not? How can you create a paradigm shift within yourself to *want* to do the will of God, so that it is a natural response rather than a constant exercise of self-discipline?

CHAPTER 7

Perhaps the skill of vision casting is what people most often associate with strong leadership. Why do you think that is? Do you think a person can be an effective leader without this skill? Why or why not?

When you read the story of the burning bush from the perspective of God trying to cast a vision, what do you learn about leadership?

Do you feel that you have caught the vision that God has cast for your life? Have you ever been aware of God calling you to a specific task? If so, how did you respond? If not, do you still take seriously the call to obey his general plan for you (i.e., to love God and others)?

To be a vision caster, a leader must know what vision to cast. What is your source of inspiration and what steps for self-evaluation do you take to ensure that you are communicating *God's* message to your followers?

When striving to cast a vision, a leader must recognize that not everyone will catch the vision. How do you prepare your heart for disappointment? How do you respond when others don't want to follow you?

David wanted to cast the vision to his people of building a temple for the Lord, but when he sought God about it, God had another plan. So David passed the baton on to another person. How good are you at trusting other people with your vision? How much delegation is proper in a good leader?

CHAPTER 8

Do you see leaders spending more time holding on to old traditions or making changes to fit new circumstances? What seems more effective to you?

Revelation 21:5 says that God is making all things new. How do you make sense of two seemingly opposing truths about God: his changelessness and his passion for making things new?

Does it sometimes seem like no matter how hard you work at things, nothing ever changes, or have you enjoyed the thrill of seeing things improve? Have you ever experienced the work of the Holy

Spirit in your organization or in your life or in the life of someone close to you, understanding that change could not have happened without his work? Explain.

How do you discern which things to hold to tightly and which things to leave open to change? Tell any stories of success or failure that you have in this area.

Accepting the need for change is one thing; actually letting the change happen is even harder. How have you been influential in making all things new?

Making changes is one thing; embracing huge life-shifts is even harder. Have you ever had an experience like Abram, where you made a radical change in your life in obedience to God? If so, what happened? If not, how do you think you would respond?

CHAPTER 9

Most leaders are aware that they need to make good decisions. How have you seen leaders come to form their decisions (e.g., using emotion, listening to advisers, praying, listing pros and cons)? Describe how the decision-making process affects their ability to lead.

Does it surprise you to discover in Scripture times that God changed his mind because he listened to his people? What does that tell you about leadership?

When you pray, do you find that God listens to you? If so, how does that make you feel? When the people you lead ask you to change your mind, do you seriously consider their requests?

Scripture makes it clear that we are to do nothing independently of God. How do you come to discern what God is telling you?

When you have made a decision, how do you communicate and implement it? How do people respond? How does their response affect you?

Nehemiah displayed remarkable perseverance. How do you think his process of decision-making affected his ability to stick with his task despite the hurdles? What does that teach you about leadership?

CHAPTER 10

Problem solving often means confronting a difficult situation, and most people are not comfortable with confrontation. Can you name any leaders who have handled this especially well? What did they do?

Scripture tells of the impossible situation humans faced when sin entered the world; it also tells of God's incredible answer. Do you ever take time to appreciate God for his leadership skills? Why or why not?

Have you ever turned to God to help you solve the problems you face? If so, what happened? If not, what is keeping you from doing so? Would you be more likely to turn to him for big problems or little problems? Why?

Why do you think people take time and energy to solve problems that could be left alone or solved by others? How do you discern which problems to tackle?

As a leader, do you ever consider yourself "above" certain situations? How can you increase compassion for others so that their problems become yours?

Nehemiah knew the great projects from the lesser concerns. Have you ever been in a situation where you had to give up a smaller thing for the sake of a bigger goal? How do you tend to handle that kind of pressure?

CHAPTER 11

Do you know of leaders who succeed because of whom they include in their team? Why do you think that makes them successful?

Scripture says that "you also were included in Christ" (Ephesians 1:13). What does God see in humans that would make him want to include them in his eternal plan? What does his patience with imperfect people teach you about leadership?

When you consider how it feels to be included in God's plan, what does that motivate you to do? Why do people want to excel when others believe in them?

As a leader, do you intentionally work to assure your team that you are one of them? Why or why not? How could you improve in this area?

How does leadership in business differ from leadership in ministry? How is it the same?

Jesus carefully chose his team, and still one of his followers betrayed him. How did Jesus handle the betrayal? What can we learn from him?

CHAPTER 12

Name some leaders in your life who have been recognized for their communication skills. Reflect on how they communicate, to determine whether it is really their speaking or their listening skills that make the difference.

God communicates with us primarily through Scripture. Name some other ways God speaks to us. What does his communication style teach us about him? about leadership?

Do you think of the Bible as a letter to us from God? A letter comes only from an acquaintance. How acquainted are you with God? Do you think the Word would become more personal to you if you spent more time getting to know God?

How much attention do you pay to the words you speak? What do you think would happen if you took a week to record every word you spoke? Would you see people uplifted or otherwise?

The words that come out of our mouths reflect the attitudes of our hearts. What do your words reflect about you? Why is it especially important for a leader to have attitudes of the heart in check?

Jesus communicated his message via parables. What were the risks in using this form of communication? What were the benefits?

CHAPTER 13

How have you seen people effectively encourage others to great things even in the midst of despair? What does this teach you about leadership?

Why did God continue to pursue his people in the Old Testament stories? If you have ever considered building others up an obstacle to building yourself up, does contemplating God's ways change your mind at all? Why or why not?

Can you think of someone who took time to encourage you through a difficult situation? How did he or she display attributes of God? leadership qualities?

Do you believe that the more you encourage others, the more satisfaction you find in your own life? Why or why not? Do you have stories to back up your belief?

Have you ever found yourself the main support person for someone who needed encouragement? How did you handle it? What was the result? What did you learn about the value of encouragement for the receiver and the giver?

If anyone can say he has faced hardships, it's the apostle Paul. And yet he continued to expend intense energy to encourage others. Does that motivate you to keep going through your hard times, and to encourage others in the midst of your own troubles? Why or why not? What can you do to grow in this area?

CHAPTER 14

Exhorters are people who spur others on to higher levels of achievement. Do you think leaders can exhort without confrontation? Why or why not?

People often think of God as our loving Father (which is accurate), while forgetting his perfect holiness. What Scripture passages or biblical stories help you to accept, even to welcome, God's discipline?

Have you ever experienced exhortation from God? How did you handle it at the time? as you look back? What does God's style of exhortation teach you about leadership?

Do you have a tendency to seek out a place devoid of conflict? If so, is it effective? Why or why not? How can you maintain peace even in the midst of conflict? How can you exude that peace to others?

When you are in a position that requires you to exhort, how do you handle it? How do you balance compassion with discipline?

Paul is a biblical hero whom readers of the Bible know well. How does his personality allow him to exhort with authority? What does that teach you about your own life as a leader?

CHAPTER 15

When you are selecting leaders through voting or hiring or delegating, do you find yourself secretly (or not so secretly) including likeability in the list of requirements? Do you think there is any value in doing this? Why or why not?

Do you agree that the Bible is all about relationship? Why or why not? Do you think of God as a God of rules or relationship? What experiences formed that opinion?

What analogies would you use to describe your relationship with God (i.e., father/child, friend/friend, master/servant, husband/wife, etc.)? Considering that God is ultimately your leader, what do the various levels of relationship you experience with him teach you about leadership?

Do you find yourself fearful of building relationships with the people you lead? Why or why not? How can you build relationships in a healthy way?

Do you tend to be an introvert or an extrovert? How does that affect your relationship-building skills? How can you learn to depend on others without becoming codependent?

Hosea was called into a relationship that was extremely difficult. What can you learn from his leadership and from his acceptance of leadership?

CHAPTER 16

Servant-leadership is a buzzword these days, but what would you say a true servant leader looks like? Do you know any servant leaders who are in the limelight? Why do you think that is?

Scripture vividly describes the agony Christ went through to complete his calling, and Christ accepted the pain without question. Would you consider that action a premier example of what servant-leadership is? Why or why not?

Jesus was able to be a servant because he understood who he was and where he was going. How does his willingness to serve in such a profound way affect your desire to follow him? How does it affect your willingness to serve others?

Do you agree that "service is not the path to greatness; service *is* greatness"? If so, are your actions matching up with your beliefs? If not, what connotations does servanthood have for you and why?

Accepting servanthood may certainly lead to suffering. Would you expect persecution to get in the way of a leader's calling or do you believe leaders are called to servanthood even more than others? Explain.

Jesus led in such a way that none who came into contact with him remained unchanged. Is this something that you want people to say about you? Why or why not? How can you be a leader who changes lives?

■

1. C. S. Lewis, *Prince Caspian* (New York: Collier/Macmillan, 1985), 136.

The Author

KENNETH BOA is engaged in a ministry of relational evangelism and discipleship, teaching, writing, and speaking. He holds a B.S. from Case Institute of Technology, a Th.M. from Dallas Theological Seminary, a Ph.D. from New York University, and a D.Phil. from the University of Oxford in England.

Dr. Boa is president of Reflections Ministries, an organization that seeks to encourage, teach, and equip people to know Christ, follow him, become progressively conformed to his image, and reproduce his life in others. He is also president of Trinity House Publishers, a publishing company that is dedicated to the creation of tools to help people manifest eternal values in a temporal arena by drawing them to intimacy with God and a better understanding of the culture in which they live.

Recent publications by Dr. Boa include *Conformed to His Image, 20 Compelling Evidences that God Exists, Face to Face, Augustine to Freud*, and *Faith Has Its Reasons*. He is a contributing editor to *The Open Bible* and *The Leadership Bible*, and the consulting editor of the *Zondervan NASB Study Bible*.

Kenneth Boa also writes a free monthly teaching letter called *Reflections*. If you would like to be on the mailing list, visit www.reflectionsministries.org or call 800-DRAW NEAR (800-372-9632).